# YOUCAT

## Youth Prayer Book

Hannah,
God bless you on your
Confirmation Day!
May 22, 2014
Our Lady of Sorrows

ihs
יהוה

# YOUCAT

ENGLISH

## YOUTH PRAYER BOOK

Edited by

Fr. Georg von Lengerke

and

Dörte Schrömges

Translated by Frank Davidson

IGNATIUS PRESS SAN FRANCISCO

Original German Edition:
YOUCAT (Deutsch) Jugendgebetbuch



*Nihil Obstat*: Reverend Monsignor J. Warren Holleran, S. T. D.
*Imprimatur*: † Most Reverend Salvatore J. Cordileone, Archbishop of San Francisco
December 11, 2012

Cover design, layout, illustrations, and typesetting: Alexander von Lengerke, Cologne
Coordination with publisher: Bernhard Meuser



**Symbols and their meaning:**

 Citation from Sacred Scripture

 Quotations from various authors, including saints and other Christian authors

 Definitions See the definition given for the term.


ISBN 978-1-58617-703-4
Library of Congress Control Number 2012933892
Printed in the United States of America
20 19 18 17 16 15 14 13 12 11 10 9 8 7 6 5 4 3 2

## CONTENTS

# You can pray

You can pray. Maybe you have not prayed since you were a child. Maybe praying is still something completely unfamiliar to you. Or someone told you that it is difficult to pray or that it would do no good anyway. Perhaps you are afraid that God would not hear your prayer. Or you have heard about great feelings that can be experienced during prayer and you are afraid of being disappointed. But all that must not prevent you from praying.

**Take a small step!**

You can pray. We can tell you that, although we do not know you personally at all. But the One to whom you can pray and who wants to speak to you knows you. He is quite close to you. He knows you better than you know yourself and is closer to you than you are to yourself. Jesus is God, who has become man. And already when he came into the world he decided to dwell in your heart too. He is waiting there for you. He wants to be sought and found there. He wants to speak to you there and to be heard by you. He knows you and loves you as no one else does. You can entrust your whole life to him, with all that is beautiful and difficult in it, with your joys and your sorrows, with what makes you happy, and with what is unsightly and makes you ashamed.

Praying means entrusting yourself to God with everything. Praying means being silent and listening. And it means letting him into your daily life, into your flesh and your memory, into everything that you say, think, and do. God has already taken the big step toward you. The path into prayer begins for you with only a small step. We invite you to take it.

## The two-week prayer book and the life themes

This book is supposed to help you on this prayer path of friendship with God. It is a collection of old and new prayers for good and bad days and nights. You will find in it prayers from Sacred Scripture and prayers of experienced people of prayer from history and of people living today.

The book consists of two parts. The first part is a prayer cycle with morning and evening prayers for two weeks. The days of the first week are dedicated to themes from our life with God and those of the second week to themes from God's life with us. The second part is a collection of prayers about various topics and concerns. They can be combined with the regular rhythm of the first part and be fit into it – depending on the occasion, the various liturgical seasons of the Church, or your concerns.

## The prayers of others are a way into your prayer

The preformulated prayers can lead you into praying in your own words and into the interior prayer of silence. The preformulated prayers, after all, are not there just to "recite". When you make the prayer of another person your own, then you pray together with him and he prays with you. The authors of the prayers in this book want to pray with you and for you. They can become companions on the way of faith who help you to find more and more your own words and also the silence of prayer. So you increasingly become a praying person who is united with God.

It may be that an individual prayer, sentence, or word strikes deep into your heart. Then linger there. Take your time. Let the word sink into the depths of your heart and into your soul. You might like to learn it by heart and to take it with you into the projects and concerns of your day. You may find it helpful to pray some prayers aloud. You do not always have to say all of the prayers either. Be selective, and stay with it when a text speaks to you in a special way.

While we were seeking, finding, and also praying these prayers again and again, we followed the same path that you can take with this book. And we keep following it with you. And with us countless other praying people are walking: people from all times since the creation of the world, those who are already with God, and those who are still living with us today. Many are praying with you and for you – and we are, too. You can pray. And if you want, you can begin today.

Ehreshoven, August 2011
Father Georg Lengerke and Dörte Schrömges

## Little school of prayer

### Make the decision.

God willed and created us to be free human persons. Many times a day we deliberate, set priorities, make decisions. Without decisions nothing gets done. If you want to, make the decision to become a praying person and to shape your relationship to God. Decide deliberately ahead of time: I will pray at such and such a time. In the evening make the decision to pray the morning prayer and in the morning to pray the evening prayer.

### Be faithful in little things.

Many begin to pray with great resolutions. After a while they fail and think that they could not pray at all. Begin with definite short prayer times. And keep doing it faithfully. Then your longing and your prayer, too, can grow, as it is appropriate for you, your time, and the circumstances.

> The most important part of praying correctly is doing it regularly. That means not only when your heart impels you. The soul lives on prayer. But all life requires regularity and repetition, a rhythm.
>
> ROMANO GUARDINI

### Take time to pray.

Praying means being alert to the fact that God is interested in you. With him you do not have to schedule appointments. There are three criteria for the time of your prayer that can be helpful. Choose set times (habit helps), quiet times (this is often early morning and in the evening), and valuable time that you like but are willing to give away as a gift (no "spare moments").

> "We can pray at any time." I know that we can, but I fear that generally those who do not pray at set times seldom pray.
>
> CHARLES HADDON SPURGEON

## Prepare a place.

4

The place where you pray has its effect on your praying. Therefore look for a place where you can pray well. For many people this will be at the bedside or the desk. Others find it helpful when they have a specially prepared place that reminds and invites them: a stool or a chair with a kneeler, a carpet, an icon or picture, a candle, the Bible, a prayer book.

> But when you pray, go into your room and shut the door and pray to your Father who is in secret.
>
> MATTHEW 6:6

## Rituals give structure to your prayer life.

5

Getting over inertia every time so as to pray can be a great expense of energy. Give your prayer a fixed order (a ritual). This is not supposed to restrict you but rather to help you, so that you do not have to deliberate every day whether and how you want to pray. Before prayer place yourself consciously in the presence of God; after prayer take another moment to thank God for his blessings and to place yourself under his protection.

> The prayer that a person prays to the best of his ability has great power. It makes a bitter heart sweet, a sad heart glad, a poor heart rich, a foolish heart wise, a timid heart bold, a weak heart strong; it makes a blind heart see and a cold heart burn. It draws the great God into the little heart; it carries the hungry soul upward to God, the living source, and brings two lovers together: God and the soul.
>
> SAINT GERTRUDE THE GREAT

## Let the whole person pray.

Praying is accomplished not only in thoughts and words. In prayer your whole person can be united with God: your body, your internal and external perception, your memory, your will, your thoughts and feelings or the dream from last night. Even distractions often give you important information about what really concerns and motivates you and what you can intentionally bring into God's presence and leave with him. When things to be done that you do not want to forget occur to you while praying, you can just write them down and then go back to praying.

> ❞ When your mind wanders or gives way to distractions, gently recall it and place it once more close to its Divine Master. If you should do nothing else but repeat this during the whole time of prayer, your hour would be very well spent and you would perform a spiritual exercise most acceptable to God.
>
> SAINT FRANCIS DE SALES

## Pray in a variety of ways.

Discover and practice the many ways of praying, which can vary depending on the time, one's frame of mind, and the situation at the moment: a prayer composed by someone else with which I join in; personal prayer about my own concerns; praying with a passage from Sacred Scripture (for example the readings for the day); the prayer of the heart (or "Jesus Prayer"), in which a short prayer formula or just the name "Jesus" is repeated with each breath; interior prayer, in which the whole person is silent and listens internally and externally.

## Use the opportunities.

You can also make use of the opportunities that arise to pray at in-between times (for example, short fervent prayers, a petition, a prayer of thanksgiving or praise): while waiting; while riding on the bus, the train, or in the car (instead of turning the music on right away); during free time; while visiting a chapel or church along your daily walk. Let the opportunities that you have to pray become invitations to unite yourself again and again with God.

## Let God speak.

Praying also means listening to God's voice. God speaks most explicitly in the words of Sacred Scripture, which the Church reads day after day. He speaks through the Tradition of the Church and the witness of the saints. But he also speaks – often in a hidden way – in the heart of every man, for instance, in the judgment of your conscience or through an interior joy. God's word in Scripture makes it possible to hear the word of God in the heart and lends a voice to it. Give God a chance to speak in your prayer. Become familiar with him, so that you can learn to tell his voice apart from the many other voices and come to know his will.

> We complain that [God] does not make Himself present to us for a few minutes we reserve for Him, but what about the twenty-three and half hours during which God may be knocking at our door and we answer "I am busy..."?
>
> ANTHONY BLOOM



## Pray with the Church on earth and in heaven.

Anyone who prays – whether alone or with others – enters into the great community of those who pray. It extends from earth to heaven and includes those who are alive today and also the angels, the saints, and the unknown multitude of those who live with God. Praying also means praying for each other. Therefore it is good to pray not just by yourself but also, when possible, with others: with your family, with friends, with your congregation – and with the saints. You can ask them for their prayers. For in God's sight the community of those who pray does not cease with death.

> Make space for prayer in your lives! To pray alone is good, although it is even more beautiful and fruitful to pray together, because the Lord assured us he would be present wherever two or three are gathered in his name (cf. Rom. 8:20).
>
> POPE BENEDICT XVI, World Youth Day 2009

# PART ONE

# 1 I will praise you day by day

**A TWO-WEEK PRAYER BOOK**

# Week One – My path with God

## YOU KNOW ME

+ In the name of the Father, and of the Son,
and of the Holy Spirit. Amen.*

(At every + make a small Sign of the Cross at the place indicated.)

**+ Lord, open my senses**

+ Lord, open my lips,
so that my mouth may proclaim your praise.

+ Lord, open my eyes,
so that I may see your works and human needs.

+ Lord, open my ears,
so that I may hear your word and the cry of the poor.

+ Lord, open my nose,
so that I can distinguish what is alive from what is dead.

+ Lord, open my understanding,
so that I may understand you and your word.

+ Lord, open my heart,
so that I may make room for you and seek and find you in all things.

+ Lord, open my hands,
so that I may receive from you and cheerfully give to people.
Amen.

! In many communities of prayer the first prayer of the day begins with the petition from Psalm 51: *"Lord, open my lips, and my mouth shall proclaim your praise."* Connected with this is the petition to be awakened to the praise of God and to be aware of the purposes for which you otherwise open your lips in the course of the day.

! * You can find a prayer to accompany the Sign of the Cross on page 105!

## I saw you

[At that time] Jesus saw Nathanael coming to him, and said of him, "Behold, an Israelite indeed, in whom is no guile!" Nathanael said to him, "How do you know me?" Jesus answered him, "Before Philip called you, when you were under the fig tree, I saw you." Nathanael answered him, "Rabbi, you are the Son of God! You are the King of Israel!"

JOHN 1:47–49

*Silence*

*My petition for the day...*

## Our Father

Try sometime to pray the Our Father with your breath. Pray one sentence each time you exhale. It is, after all, the Holy Spirit himself who is praying in you. And your breath is an image for him, and for the spirit that God gave you when he gave life to you (cf. GENESIS 2:7).

Our Father who art in heaven,
hallowed be thy name;
thy kingdom come,
thy will be done
on earth as it is in heaven.
Give us this day our daily bread,
and forgive us our trespasses,
as we forgive those who trespass against us;
and lead us not into temptation,
but deliver us from evil.
[For the kingdom and the power
and the glory are yours for ever and ever.
Amen.]

MATTHEW 6:9-13

## Saint Patrick's Breastplate

I bind unto myself today
the strong name of the Trinity:
by invocation of the same
the Three in One and One in Three.

I bind unto myself today
the power of God to hold and lead:
his eye to watch, his might to stay,
his ear to hearken to my need;
the wisdom of my God to teach,
his hand to guide, his shield to ward;
the Word of God to give me speech,
his heavenly host to be my guard!

Christ be with me, Christ within me,
Christ behind me, Christ before me,
Christ beside me, Christ to win me,
Christ to comfort and restore me,
Christ beneath me, Christ above me,
Christ in quiet, Christ in danger,
Christ in hearts of all that love me,
Christ in mouth of friend and stranger.

I bind unto myself the name,
the strong name of the Trinity:
by invocation of the same,
the Three in One and One in Three;
of whom all nature hath creation,
eternal Father, Spirit, Word:
praise to the Lord of my salvation –
salvation is of Christ the Lord.
Amen.

SAINT PATRICK OF IRELAND

May the Lord bless me, protect me from all evil,
and bring me to everlasting life.
+ In the name of the Father, and of the Son, and of the Holy Spirit. Amen.

+ In the name of the Father, and of the Son,
and of the Holy Spirit. Amen.

*Quietly, I look back over this day. I call to mind the things and the people I have encountered in the course of this day and what I have thought, said, and done.*

Loving Father, I thank you for this day and for all the good things I have experienced. Forgive me, wherever I have sinned against you, against others, or against myself, and let my heart rest in peace with you. Amen.

**Praying the Psalms**
The Psalms are the prayer book of the Bible. When you pray them, you do so together with millions of Christians and Jews throughout the world – those of today and those who have prayed them over the past three thousand years – since for God every prayer that was ever spoken remains now and forever present. The Psalms can help us to bring before God every experience and every movement of the human heart – joy and thanksgiving, desperation and anger, even hatred of evil things and the anguished question: Does God sleep, while we suffer?

### I receive myself from your hands

Unceasingly, I receive myself from your hands.
This is my truth and my joy.
Unceasingly, your eye rests upon me,
and I live by your gaze,
O my Creator and my Salvation.
Teach me,
in the silence of your presence,
to understand the mystery that I am.
And the fact that I am
through you
and before you
and for you.
Amen.

ROMANO GUARDINI

The glory of God is man fully alive.

SAINT IRENAEUS OF LYONS

### You search me and you know me

O LORD, you have searched me and known me!
You know when I sit down and when I rise up;
you discern my thoughts from afar.
You search out my path and my lying down,
and are acquainted with all my ways.

Even before a word is on my tongue,
behold, O LORD, you know it altogether...
For you formed my inward parts,
you knitted me together in my mother's womb.
I praise you, for I am wondrously made.
Wonderful are your works! ...
Your eyes beheld my unformed substance;
in your book were written, every one of them,
the days that were formed for me,
when as yet there was none of them.
How precious to me are your thoughts, O God!
How vast is the sum of them!
[Glory be to the Father, and to the Son,
and to the Holy Spirit,
as it was in the beginning, is now, and ever shall be,
world without end. Amen.]

PSALM 139:1–4, 13, 14, 16, 17

**I adore you**

Lord, you have made us for yourself,
and our hearts are restless
until they find rest in you.
Yours is the light of day,
yours is the darkness of night.
I too am yours and I adore you.
Let me rest in peace,
bless the coming day,
and let me awake
to praise your Name. Amen.

SAINT AUGUSTINE OF HIPPO, adapted

Grant me, Lord, a quiet night
and a perfect end in you.
+ In the name of the Father, and of the Son, and of the Holy Spirit. Amen.

## YOU HAVE MADE MY FOOTSTEPS FIRM

+ In the name of the Father, and of the Son,
and of the Holy Spirit. Amen.

> What matters above all is to make a determined beginning. A person who begins with determination already has a good part of the journey behind him.
>
> SAINT TERESA OF AVILA

### I am yours

I am not afraid, my LORD,
for you have created me.
You call me by my name.
I am yours!
When I pass through the waters, you are with me,
and through rivers – they shall not overwhelm me.
When I walk through fire I shall not be burned,
and the flame shall not consume me.
For you are the LORD my God,
The Holy One, my Savior!
I am precious in your sight,
and you love me.
For your glory you have created,
formed and fashioned each one by your name.
You alone are God,
now and for evermore.
Since you are by me, I do not fear.

Based on ISAIAH 43:1–7

## He will establish and strengthen you

Cast all your anxieties on him, for he cares about you... knowing that the same experience of suffering is required of your brotherhood throughout the world. And after you have suffered a little while, the God of all grace, who has called you to his eternal glory in Christ, will himself restore, establish, and strengthen you.

1 PETER 5:7, 9–10

*Silence*

*My petition for the day...*

Our Father...

> Whoever wants to start a good life should do so like someone setting out a circle. If he has fixed the center of the circle accurately, and it remains firm, then the line of the circle will be a good one. In other words, a person should first learn to set his heart firmly in God, and then he will be constant in all his works.
>
> MEISTER ECKHART

## My longing for truth

For the longing for truth
that you have planted deep within me.
It is not going to be fobbed off
with empty promises,
simplistic solutions,
or hollow phrases.

I ask you, my Father,
to help me look at the truth of my own life,
at all that is genuine and all that is false,
at all that is true and all the lies,
at all the fullness and all the emptiness.

I trust in you, my Father,
to come into my life
and brighten my darkness with your light,
and be for me the Truth
that will fill all my longing.
Amen.

DÖRTE SCHRÖMGES

May the Lord bless me, protect me from all evil,
and bring me to everlasting life.
+ In the name of the Father, and of the Son, and of the Holy Spirit. Amen.

+ In the name of the Father, and of the Son, and of the Holy Spirit. Amen.

*Quietly, I look back over this day. I call to mind the things and the people I have encountered in the course of this day and what I have thought, said, and done.*

Loving Father, I thank you for this day and for all the good things I have experienced. Forgive me, wherever I have sinned against you, against others, or against myself and let my heart rest in peace with you. Amen.

> What is the worst thing a person can do to himself? – to forget that he is the son of a King.
>
> MARTIN BUBER

**Lord, my God, I rejoice**

Lord, my God,
just as the fish cannot live without water,
so I cannot live without you.
You have created me;
you uphold my life.

Today I come to thank you
for the life that you give me, each day anew.
I come to thank you,
and to tell you how much I love life.

Yes, I love to be alive,
even if I am often not quite myself,
when I seem to be going nowhere
and don't know where my life is taking me.

Above all, I rejoice to be your child,
to breathe the life of God within me,
your Holy Spirit.
You want to live in me,
to be a guest within me.
With all my heart I thank you
for this honor, for this joy.
Amen.

Based on a prayer from Upper Volta

God does not desire *sacrifice and offering;* that is, he does not want you to give something that belongs to you. He is not asking for your achievements and successes, however laudable they may be; nor does he want your good grades or the things that make you important in the eyes of others. What he longs for is *you yourself*, your very heart, just as it is today. He also wants you to hand over to him all your hurt and your guilt. Then he will be your Savior and heal what is broken in you.

**I come to do your will**

He inclined to me and heard my cry.
He drew me up from the desolate pit,
out of the miry bog,
and set my feet upon a rock,
making my steps secure.
He put a new song in my mouth,
a song of praise to our God....
You have multiplied, O LORD my God,
your wondrous deeds and your thoughts toward us;
none can compare with you!
Were I to proclaim and tell of them,
they would be more than can be numbered.
Sacrifice and offering you do not desire;
but you have given me an open ear.
Burnt offering and sin offering
you have not required.
Then I said, "Behold, I come;...
I delight to do your will, O my God;
your law is within my heart."
[Glory be to the Father, and to the Son,
and to the Holy Spirit,
as it was in the beginning, is now, and ever shall be,
world without end. Amen.]

PSALM 40:1–3, 5–8

> God no more takes his eyes off us than does a mother take them off her child who is just starting to walk.
>
> SAINT JEAN-MARIE VIANNEY, Curé of Ars

**Prayer of blessing**

Lord, be before me
and show me the right path.
Lord, be beside me
and protect me.
Lord, be behind me
and preserve me from the malice of evil men.
Lord, be beneath me,
save me from the snare
and catch me when I fall.
Lord, be within me
and comfort me when I am sad.
Lord, be around me
and defend me from those who assail me.
Lord, be above me
and bless me.

Lord, grant me a quiet night and a perfect end in you.
+ In the name of the Father, and of the Son,
and of the Holy Spirit. Amen.

## YOU ARE THE WAY

+ In the name of the Father, and of the Son, and of the Holy Spirit. Amen.

### From your loving hands

Lord, may this day, and all that it brings,
come to me from your loving hands.
For you are the Way, the Truth, and the Life.
You are the Way, let me just follow.
You are the Truth, let me just see.
You are the Life, let it enfold me,
in summer and winter,
in sunshine and sorrow.
All's good that you send me,
today and tomorrow.
Let me just love you, and do as you say.
And so in your name I set out on this day.
Amen.

From an ancient German pilgrim prayer

## I am the way

Thomas said to him [Jesus], "Lord, we do not know where you are going; how can we know the way?" Jesus said to him [Thomas], "I am the way, and the truth, and the life; no one comes to the Father, but by me."

JOHN 14:5–6

*Silence*

*My petition for the day...*

Our Father...

> Therein lies the nobility of the Faith – that we have the heart to dare something.
>
> BLESSED JOHN HENRY NEWMAN

## Leaning on you, I venture forth

Heavenly Father,
be our Salvation.
Grant that I may leave my poverty behind
and, leaning upon you,
may venture forth
on the unknown oceans of freedom.
Amen.

TEILHARD DE CHARDIN

May the Lord bless me, protect me from all evil,
and bring me to everlasting life.
+ In the name of the Father, and of the Son,
and of the Holy Spirit. Amen.

+ In the name of the Father, and of the Son,
and of the Holy Spirit. Amen.

*Quietly, I look back over this day. I call to mind the things and the people I have encountered in the course of this day and what I have thought, said, and done.*

Loving Father, I thank you for this day and for all the good things I have experienced. Forgive me, wherever I have sinned against you, against others, or against myself and let my heart rest in peace with you. Amen.

Jesus spoke to them, saying, "I am the light of the world; he who follows me will not walk in darkness, but will have the light of life."

JOHN 8:12

**Lead, Kindly Light**

Lead, Kindly Light, amid the encircling gloom
Lead Thou me on!
The night is dark, and I am far from home –
Lead Thou me on!
Keep Thou my feet; I do not ask to see
The distant scene – one step enough for me

I was not ever thus, nor pray'd that Thou
Shouldst lead me on.
I loved to choose and see my path, but now
Lead Thou me on!
I loved the garish day, and, spite of fears,
Pride ruled my will: remember not past years.

So long Thy power hath blest me, sure it still
Will lead me on,
O'er moor and fen, o'er crag and torrent, till
The night is gone;
And with the morn those angel faces smile
Which I have loved long since, and lost awhile.

BLESSED JOHN HENRY NEWMAN

*False gods* are all those powers, demands, and expectations, all the trends, fashions, and siren voices that whisper to us, "I am your God! Follow me and do what I say, then I will make you happy!" This Psalm reminds us that God alone is God; he alone has the power to make us free and happy.

### You show me the path of life

Preserve me, O God, for in you I take refuge.
I say to the Lord, "You are my Lord;
I have no good apart from you."...
Those who choose another god multiply their sorrows;
their libations of blood I will not pour out
or take their names upon my lips....
Therefore my heart is glad, and my soul rejoices;
my body also dwells secure.
For you do not give me up to Sheol,
or let your godly one see the Pit.
You show me the path of life;
in your presence there is fulness of joy,
in your right hand are pleasures for evermore.
[Glory be to the Father and to the Son
and to the Holy Spirit,
as it was in the beginning, is now, and ever shall be,
world without end. Amen.]

PSALM 16:1, 2, 4, 9–11

### Searching

Father,
I am searching,
I make no assertions.
But you, my God,
watch over my steps
and show me the way.
Amen.

SAINT AUGUSTINE OF HIPPO

Lord, grant me a quiet night
and a perfect end in you.
+ In the name of the Father, and of the Son, and of the Holy Spirit. Amen.

## WALKING IN YOUR NAME

+ In the name of the Father, and of the Son,
and of the Holy Spirit. Amen.

> As often as you begin any good work, pray first of all fervently that God may bring it to completion.
>
> From the Rule of SAINT BENEDICT OF NURSIA

### O God, I adore you

O Wisdom that conceived me,
O Will that desired me,
O Power that created me,
O Grace that raised me,
O Voice that calls me,
O Word that speaks to me,
O Kindness that enriches me,
O Providence that guides me,
O Mercy that pardons me,
O Love that surrounds me,
O Spirit that enlivens me,
O Peace that fills me,
O Holiness that transforms me –
May I never rest until I see you.
O God, I adore you. Amen.

From the GOTTESLOB, the German Catholic hymn and prayer book

### I send you out

[Jesus sent out the twelve apostles, telling them,] "Preach as you go, saying, 'The kingdom of heaven is at hand.' Heal the sick, raise the dead, cleanse lepers, cast out demons. You received without pay, give without pay.... Behold, I send you out as sheep in the midst of wolves; so be wise as serpents and innocent as doves."

MATTHEW 10:7–8, 16

*Silence*

*My petition for the day...*

Our Father...

> Lord, to whom shall we go? You have the words of eternal life.
>
> Saint Peter in JOHN 6:68

**Make us worthy to serve**

Make us worthy, Lord
to serve our fellow men
throughout the world
who live and die
in poverty and hunger.
Give them through our hands this day
their daily bread,
and by our understanding love,
give peace and joy.

> **The simple way**
> The fruit of silence is prayer.
> The fruit of prayer is faith.
> The fruit of faith is love.
> The fruit of love is service.
>
> BLESSED TERESA OF CALCUTTA

... Lord, grant that I may seek rather
to comfort than to be comforted;
to understand
than to be understood;
to love
than to be loved;
for it is by forgetting self
that one finds,
it is by forgiving
that one is forgiven,
it is by dying
that one awakens to eternal life.
Amen.

Prayers of POPE PAUL VI and SAINT FRANCIS OF ASSISI used by the Missionaries of Charity

May the Lord bless me, protect me from all evil,
and bring me to everlasting life.
+ In the name of the Father, and of the Son,
and of the Holy Spirit. Amen.

+ In the name of the Father, and of the Son, and of the Holy Spirit. Amen.

*Quietly, I look back over this day. I call to mind the things and the people I have encountered in the course of this day and what I have thought, said, and done.*

Loving Father, I thank you for this day and for all the good things I have experienced. Forgive me, wherever I have sinned against you, against others, or against myself and let my heart rest in peace with you. Amen.

**O Lord, deliver us**

O Lord, deliver us
for the sea is so great
and our boat is so small!
Amen.

Breton Fisherman's Prayer

**Word in the night**

Your word is a lamp to my feet
and a light to my path.

PSALM 119:105

**Watch, O Lord, with those who wake...**

Watch, O Lord, with those who wake...
or watch, or weep tonight,
and give your angels and saints charge
over those who sleep.
Tend your sick ones, O Lord Jesus Christ,
rest your weary ones, bless your dying ones,
soothe your suffering ones,
pity your afflicted ones,
shield your joyous ones.
And all for your love's sake. Amen.

SAINT AUGUSTINE OF HIPPO

Lord, grant me a quiet night
and a perfect end in you.
+ In the name of the Father, and of the Son,
and of the Holy Spirit. Amen.

## YOU CALL US FRIENDS

> After reflecting on their importance and reacting profoundly to them, make the effort to learn one or two prayers by heart. In this way you will be better able to direct the attention of your spirit steadily towards God. You will see for yourself how beneficial this is. Having learned these prayers by heart, you can be sure that they will be with you at all times and in all circumstances – and this is very important.
>
> SAINT THEOPHAN THE RECLUSE

+ In the name of the Father, and of the Son, and of the Holy Spirit. Amen.

### Now that the daylight fills the sky

Now that the daylight fills the sky
We lift our hearts to God on high,
That he, in all we do or say,
Would keep us free from harm today.

May he restrain our tongues from strife,
And shield from anger's din our life,
And guard with watchful care our eyes
From earth's absorbing vanities.

O may our inmost hearts be pure,
From thoughts of folly kept secure,
And pride of sinful flesh subdued
Through sparing use of daily food.

So we, when this day's work is o'er,
And shades of night return once more,
Our path of trial safely trod,
Shall give the glory to our God. Amen.

Attributed to SAINT AMBROSE OF MILAN

## I chose you

[Jesus said to his disciples,] "No longer do I call you servants, for the servant does not know what his master is doing; but I have called you friends, for all that I have heard from my Father I have made known to you. You did not choose me, but I chose you and appointed you that you should go and bear fruit and that your fruit should abide; so that whatever you ask the Father in my name, he may give it to you. This I command you, to love one another."

JOHN 15:15–17

*Silence*

*My petition for the day...*

Our Father...

> The fact that we are to gain as a friend the One who makes all things friendly makes us realize just how unfriendly things are in and around ourselves; and so we reflect again on the Friend, from whom we may ask whatever it is that we ourselves do not have, and yet must have, if the friendliness of this Friend is to lastingly light up our lives. So we set out toward God; so we ask, so we seek, so we knock on the door.
>
> HEINRICH SPAEMANN

> **"Just for today"** We pray these words, not because the future is of no importance to us, but because we must live in the here and now. What we must not do is to seek refuge in yesterday or tomorrow: "Therefore do not be anxious about tomorrow, for tomorrow will be anxious for itself. Let the day's own trouble be sufficient for the day" (MATTHEW 6:34).

## My song for today

My life is but an instant, a passing hour.
My life is but a day that escapes and flies away.
O my God! You know that to love you on earth
I only have today!...

Oh, I love you, Jesus! My soul yearns for you.
For just one day remain my sweet support.
Come reign in my heart, give me your smile
Just for today!

Lord, what does it matter if the future is gloomy?
To pray for tomorrow, oh no, I cannot!...
Keep my heart pure, cover me with your shadow
Just for today.

O Divine Pilot! whose hand guides me,
I'm soon to see you on the eternal shore.
Guide my little boat over the stormy waves in peace
Just for today.

SAINT THÉRÈSE OF LISIEUX

May the Lord bless me, protect me from all evil,
and bring me to everlasting life.
+ In the name of the Father, and of the Son,
and of the Holy Spirit. Amen.

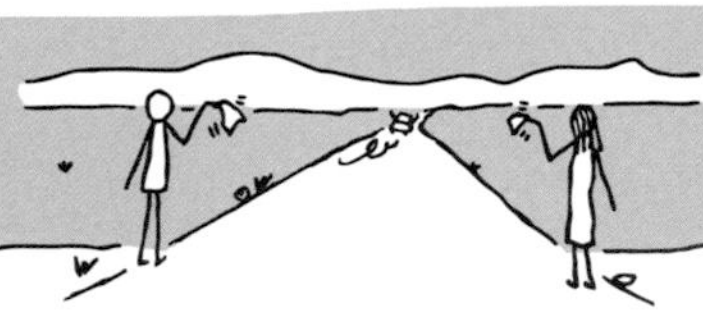

+ In the name of the Father, and of the Son,
and of the Holy Spirit. Amen.

*Quietly, I look back over this day. I call to mind the things and the people I have encountered in the course of this day and what I have thought, said, and done.*

Loving Father, I thank you for this day and for all the good things I have experienced. Forgive me, wherever I have sinned against you, against others, or against myself and let my heart rest in peace with you. Amen.

> Prayer in my opinion is nothing else than an intimate sharing between friends; it means taking time frequently to be alone with him who we know loves us.
>
> SAINT TERESA OF AVILA

**Be my Rock**

Jesus, my Lord, my God become Man,
when everything slides and so much is lost,
be then my Rock, on which I can stand.
When everything trembles
and earth seems to shake,
be my safe Refuge, unshakeably strong.
When strife surges round me
and my nearest leave me,
be then the Peace that reigns in my heart.
When I mistrust even myself
and the kind words of others,
be then Word of the Father, in whom I can trust.
When everyone leaves, and fear makes me faithless,
be then my Friend, who stays to the end.
Amen.

GEORG LENGERKE

## You alone make me dwell in safety

Answer me when I call, O God of my right!
You have given me room when I was in distress.
Be gracious to me, and hear my prayer....
There are many who say, "Oh that we might see some good!
Lift up the light of your countenance upon us, O LORD!"
You have put more joy in my heart
than they have when their grain and wine abound.
In peace I will both lie down and sleep;
for you alone, O LORD, make me dwell in safety.
[Glory be to the Father, and to the Son,
and to the Holy Spirit,
as it was in the beginning, is now, and ever shall be,
world without end. Amen.]

PSALM 4:1, 6–8

## Even before we seek you

My God, even before we seek you,
you are with us.
Before we know your name,
You are already our God.

Open our hearts to the mystery
into which we are drawn –
that you loved us first,
and so we can be happy with you.

It is not because we are good
that we can come close to you –
but because you are God.
Amen.

Lord, grant me a quiet night
and a perfect end in you.
+ In the name of the Father, and of the Son,
and of the Holy Spirit. Amen.

## YOU HEAR ME CALLING

+ In the name of the Father, and of the Son,
and of the Holy Spirit. Amen.

> When the time comes and we cannot pray, it is very simple – let Jesus pray in us to the Father in the silence of our hearts. If we cannot speak, He will speak. If we cannot pray, He will pray. So let us give Him our inability and our nothingness.
>
> BLESSED TERESA OF CALCUTTA

### I am nothing without you

God – I speak your Name
into the darkness,
into the darkness of my fear,
into the blackness of my guilt,
into the poverty of my questions and doubts.
God – in this Name
I place all my trust,
my hope of loving security,
my yearning for a *You*,
my burning desire to belong.
God – your Name rings in my ear,
with warm familiarity.
Within me my loneliness responds to You;
within me the lost child responds to You,
within me responds the poor nothing that I am.
For when I inquire into myself,
It is you that I find;
when I lose my way,
it is you that I miss.
I am nothing without you.
Amen.

ALFONS HÖFER

## The Spirit intercedes for us

Likewise the Spirit helps us in our weakness; for we do not know how to pray as we ought, but the Spirit himself intercedes for us with sighs too deep for words. And he who searches the hearts of men knows what is the mind of the Spirit, because the Spirit intercedes for the saints according to the will of God. We know that in everything God works for good.

ROMANS 8:26–28

*Silence*

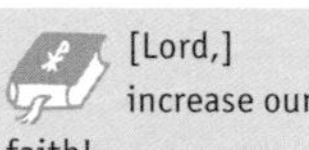

[Lord,] increase our faith!

The apostles, after Jesus spoke to them about forgiveness, LUKE 17:5

*My petition for the day...*

Our Father...

## What you will

Lord, what you will, let it be so
Where you will, there I will go
What is your will, help us to know.

Lord, when you will, the time is right,
In you there's joy in strife;
For your will I'll give my life.

To ease your burden brings no pain,
To forego all for you is gain,
As long as I in you remain.

Because you will it, it is best,
Because you will it, we are blest,
Till in your hands our hearts find rest.

BLESSED RUPERT MAYER

May the Lord bless me, protect me from all evil,
and bring me to everlasting life.
+ In the name of the Father, and of the Son,
and of the Holy Spirit. Amen.

+ In the name of the Father, and of the Son,
and of the Holy Spirit. Amen.

*Quietly, I look back over this day. I call to mind the things and the people I have encountered in the course of this day and what I have thought, said, and done.*

Loving Father, I thank you for this day and for all the good things I have experienced. Forgive me, wherever I have sinned against you, against others, or against myself and let my heart rest in peace with you. Amen.

> Even the desire to pray is already a prayer.
>
> GEORGES BERNANOS

**You do not go away**

Lord, my God,
you do not go away from those who go away from you.
How can anyone say you are an absent God?
SAINT JOHN OF THE CROSS

> I have calmed and quieted my soul, like a child quieted at its mother's breast;
> like a child that is quieted is my soul.
>
> PSALM 131:2

**You are with me**

The LORD is my shepherd, I shall not want;
he makes me lie down in green pastures.
He leads me beside still waters; he restores my soul.
He leads me in paths of righteousness for his name's sake.
Even though I walk through the valley of the shadow of death, I fear no evil; for you are with me;
your rod and your staff, they comfort me.
You prepare a table before me
in the presence of my enemies;
you anoint my head with oil, my cup overflows.
Surely goodness and mercy shall follow me
all the days of my life;
and I shall dwell in the house of the LORD for ever.
[Glory be to the Father, and to the Son,
and to the Holy Spirit,
as it was in the beginning, is now, and ever shall be,
world without end. Amen.]
PSALM 23:1–6

## You have brought this day to a close

Lord, my God, I thank you for having brought this day to a close. I thank you for granting rest to body and soul. Your hand was over me and has shielded and sustained me. Forgive all the lack of faith and all the sins of this day and help me to forgive all those who have wronged me. Let me sleep in peace beneath your sheltering hand and keep me safe from the assaults of the underworld. I commend to you all my loved ones; I commend to you this house, I commend to you my body and my soul. God, may your holy Name be praised.
Amen.

DIETRICH BONHOEFFER

Lord, grant me a quiet night
and a perfect end in you.
+ In the name of the Father, and of the Son,
and of the Holy Spirit. Amen.

## YOU KNOW WHAT I AM MADE OF

+ In the name of the Father, and of the Son,
and of the Holy Spirit. Amen.

### I let my joy fly free

Lord,
I let my joy fly free, like a bird, up to the sky.
The night has flown by, and I delight in the light.
Lord, I am happy this day, this morning.
The birds and the angels are singing, and I rejoice as well.
The universe and our hearts are open to your grace.
I feel my body alive, and give thanks.

Lord,
I delight in creation,
and the knowledge that you are behind it,
and beside, and before, and above it.
And in us too.
The Psalms sing of your love,
the prophets proclaim it,
and we experience it.

I let my joy fly free, like a bird, up to the sky.
A new day, that glistens and rustles
and rejoices with your love.
You make each day,
and each day you number
the curls on my head.
Alleluia, Lord.

From Africa

> ” I come back to the distracted thoughts that caused me such torment. For those who walk the way of prayer, it is good to have a book in hand, so that they can quickly recollect themselves again. It also helped me greatly when I looked at the fields, or at water, or flowers. These things wakened me and brought me back to a recollected state, just as well as a book.
>
> SAINT TERESA OF AVILA

### Do not be ashamed!

For this reason I remind you to rekindle the gift of God that is within you through the laying on of my hands; for God did not give us a spirit of timidity but a spirit of power and love and self-control. Do not be ashamed then of testifying to our Lord.

2 TIMOTHY 1:6–8

*Silence*

*My petition for the day...*

Our Father...

### Prayer for a watchful heart

Grant me, O Lord,
an ever-watchful heart that no alien thought
can lure away from you;
a noble heart that no base love can sully;
an upright heart that no perverse intention
can lead astray;
an invincible heart that no distress can overcome;
an unfettered heart that no impetuous desires
can enchain.
Grant me, O Lord my God,
a mind to know you,
a heart to seek you,
wisdom to find you,
conduct pleasing to you,
faithful perseverance in waiting for you,
and a hope of finally embracing you.
Amen.

SAINT THOMAS AQUINAS

May the Lord bless me, protect me from all evil,
and bring me to everlasting life.
+ In the name of the Father, and of the Son,
and of the Holy Spirit. Amen.

+ In the name of the Father, and of the Son,
and of the Holy Spirit. Amen.

*Quietly, I look back over this day. I call to mind the things and the people I have encountered in the course of this day and what I have thought, said, and done.*

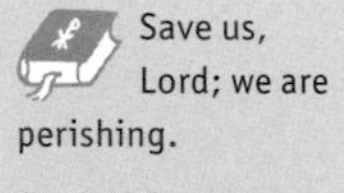

Save us, Lord; we are perishing.

The disciples in the storm, MATTHEW 8:25

Loving Father, I thank you for this day and for all the good things I have experienced. Forgive me, wherever I have sinned against you, against others, or against myself and let my heart rest in peace with you. Amen.

**You know what is best for me**

O my God, you alone are all-wise and all-knowing!
I believe that you know just what is best for me. I believe that you love me better than I love myself, that you are all-wise in your Providence and are all-powerful in your protections.
I thank you, with all my heart, that you have taken me out of my own keeping, and have bidden me to put myself in your hands. I can ask nothing better than this, to be in your care – not my own. O my Lord, through your grace, I will follow you wherever you go, and will not lead the way.
I will wait for you for your guidance, and, on obtaining it, I will act in simplicity and without fear.
And I promise that I will not be impatient, if at any time I am kept by you in darkness and perplexity; nor will I complain or fret if I come into any misfortune or anxiety. In all, I will trust in Jesus, the Lord, and my savior.
Amen.

JOHN HENRY NEWMAN

> The bended knee and the outstretched empty hands are the two primal gestures of the free human being.
>
> ALFRED DELP

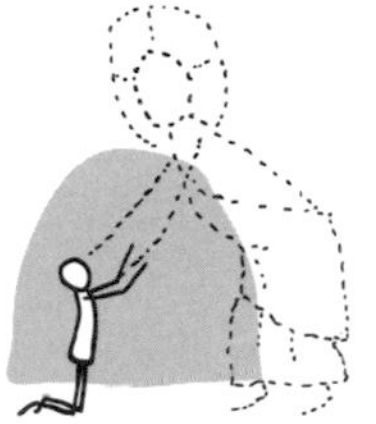

## It is good to give thanks to the Lord

It is good to give thanks to the LORD,
to sing praises to your name, O Most High;
to declare your merciful love in the morning,
and your faithfulness by night,
to the music of the lute and the harp,
to the melody of the lyre.
For you, O LORD, have made me glad by your work;
at the works of your hands I sing for joy.
How great are your works, O LORD!
Your thoughts are very deep!
The dull man cannot know,
the stupid cannot understand this...
but you, O LORD, are on high for ever.
[Glory be to the Father, and to the Son,
and to the Holy Spirit,
as it was in the beginning, is now, and ever shall be,
world without end. Amen.]

PSALM 92:1–6, 8

**To seek you is to love you**

O my God,
to depart from you is to fall,
to return to you is to rise up,
to remain in you is to build on solid ground.

To go away from you is to die,
to return to you is to be resurrected,
to dwell in you is to live.

No one loses you without being deceived,
no one seeks you without being called,
no one finds you without being purified.

To abandon you is to become lost,
to seek you is to love you,
to see you is to possess you.

Faith urges us toward you,
hope leads us to you,
love unites us with you. Amen.

SAINT AUGUSTINE OF HIPPO, adapted

Lord, grant me a quiet night
and a perfect end in you.
+ In the name of the Father, and of the Son,
and of the Holy Spirit. Amen.

# Week Two – God's path with me

## GOD ARISES – RESURRECTION

+ In the name of the Father, and of the Son, and of the Holy Spirit. Amen.

> ! When Mechthild speaks of the "mighty power" of God that "shelters" and protects her, she is saying that God's almighty power is greater than all other kinds of might and power that can be imagined. God is not merely one power among many. He is the origin of all, the source of all strength and power. This thought alone is a mighty one.

### I praise you, Lord

I praise you, Lord,
saved by your mercy.
I praise you, Lord,
honored by your humiliation.
I praise you, Lord,
led by your kindness.
I praise you, Lord,
ruled by your wisdom.
I praise you, Lord,
sheltered by your mighty power.
I praise you, Lord,
sanctified by your grace.
I praise you, Lord,
enlightened by your inner light.
I praise you, Lord,
raised up by your goodness.
Amen.

SAINT MECHTHILD OF MAGDEBURG

> Great is your day, my Lord. May it not be diminished by us.
>
> SAINT EPHREM THE SYRIAN

**I have seen the Lord**

Mary stood weeping outside the tomb, and as she wept she stooped to look into the tomb.... She turned round and saw Jesus standing, but she did not know that it was Jesus. Jesus said to her, "Woman, why are you weeping? Whom do you seek?" Supposing him to be the gardener, she said to him, "Sir, if you have carried him away, tell me where you have laid him, and I will take him away." Jesus said to her, "Mary." She turned and said to him in Hebrew, "Rab-bo'ni!" (which means Teacher). Jesus said to her, "Do not hold me, for I have not yet ascended to the Father; but go to my brethren and say to them, I am ascending to my Father and your Father, to my God and your God." Mary Magdalene went and said to the disciples, "I have seen the Lord"; and she told them that he had said these things to her.

JOHN 20:11, 14–18

*Silence*

*My petition for the day...*

Our Father...

**Rise up in me**

Risen One,
You descended
into death
and to all those
death has held buried within.

Descend also into my depths,
down to all that is dead within me,
and to everything
that still waits for your life
and your light.

You have truly risen
from the tomb
and you lead the dead into life,
the benighted into the light
and sinners to reconciliation
with the Father.

Rise up in me also,
from the tombs within me,
and raise up what is dead within me into life,
my unattractiveness into the loving gaze
and my guilt into the waiting arms
of the Father.
Amen.

GEORG LENGERKE

May the Lord bless me, protect me from all evil,
and bring me to everlasting life.
+ In the name of the Father, and of the Son,
and of the Holy Spirit. Amen.

+ In the name of the Father, and of the Son,
and of the Holy Spirit. Amen.

> "I say to you, dear young people: Do not be afraid of Christ! He takes nothing away, and he gives you everything. When we give ourselves to him, we receive a hundredfold in return. Yes, open, open wide the doors to Christ – and you will find true life.
>
> POPE BENEDICT XVI

*Quietly, I look back over this day. I call to mind the things and the people I have encountered in the course of this day and what I have thought, said, and done.*

Loving Father, I thank you for this day and for all the good things I have experienced. Forgive me, wherever I have sinned against you, against others, or against myself and let my heart rest in peace with you. Amen.

**Before we end our day**

Before we end our day, O Lord,
We make this prayer to you:
That you continue in your love
To guard your people here.

Give us this night untroubled rest
And build our strength anew;
Your splendor driving far away
All darkness of the foe.

Our hearts' desire to love you, Lord,
Watch over while we sleep,
That when the new day dawns on high
We may your praises sing.

All glory be to you, O Christ,
Who saved mankind from death –
To share with you the Father's love
And in the Spirit live.

Based on a fifth-century hymn for Compline

**You are my refuge**

Whoever dwells under your protection, Most High God,
who rests in the shadow of your Almighty power,
will say to you, "My refuge and my fortress;
my God, in whom I trust."

For you, O LORD, will deliver me from the snare of the fowler
and from the deadly pestilence;
You will cover me with your pinions,
and under your wings I will find refuge;
Your faithfulness is a shield and buckler.
I will not fear the terror of the night,
nor the arrow that flies by day,
nor the pestilence that stalks in darkness,
nor the destruction that wastes at noonday....
For you are my refuge,
the Most High is my habitation,
no evil shall befall me.....
For he will give his angels charge of me
to guard me in all my ways.
Glory be to the Father, and to the Son,
and to the Holy Spirit,
as it was in the beginning, is now, and ever shall be,
world without end. Amen.

Based on PSALM 91



All that we are, and all that we have, we can entrust to God. He begrudges us nothing. He wants us to have ownership of, and not be owned by, the things of this world. In God's hands our freedom remains free, our memory awake, our understanding enlightened, and our will sound.

**Take, O Lord**

Take, O Lord, and receive all my liberty,
my memory, my understanding,
and my entire will,
all that I have and possess.

Thou hast given all to me;
to thee, O Lord, I return it.
All is thine;
dispose of it according to thy will.

Give me thy love
and thy grace,
for this is enough for me. Amen.

IGNATIUS OF LOYOLA

Lord, grant me a quiet night
and a perfect end in you.
+ In the name of the Father, and of the Son,
and of the Holy Spirit. Amen.

## BUILT OF LIVING STONES – THE CHURCH

+ In the name of the Father, and of the Son,
and of the Holy Spirit. Amen.

**God, you walk the ways of men**

Merciful God and Father, creator of heaven and earth,
you have created man and woman in your own image.
You are close to the people of every nation
and of every age.
We praise you.
You have chosen Israel as your people
and made an enduring covenant with them.
In the fullness of time you sent Jesus, your Son,
and in him walked the ways of men.
We thank you.
In the power of the Spirit you accompany
your Church.
You bestow on her the abundance of his gifts.
She is the Church of saints and of sinners,
but you remain true to her on the way
into the third millennium.
We trust in you.
Let your Kingdom become tangible even in our time –
through truth and love among men,
through justice and peace between nations.
We ask you this through Jesus Christ,
our brother and Lord.
Amen.

BLESSED JOHN PAUL II

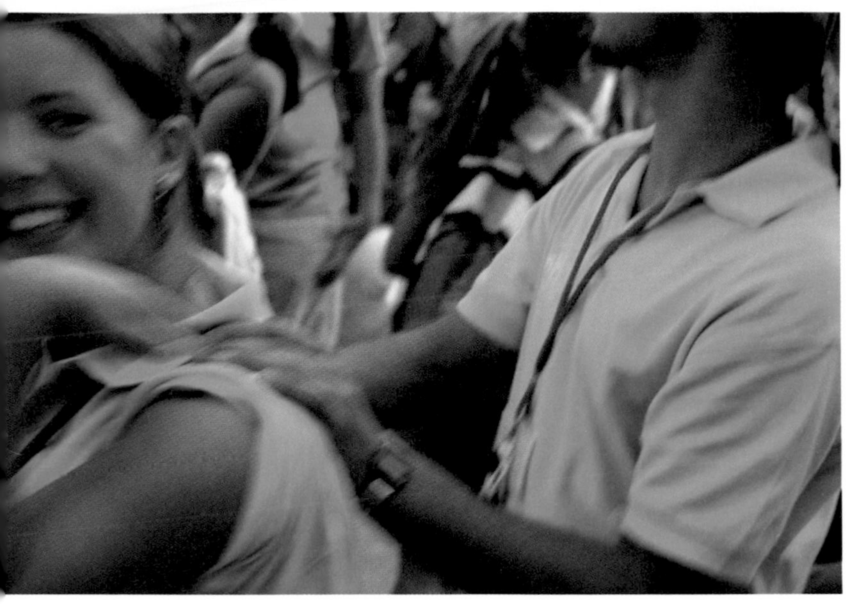

> God leads us by strange ways; we know He wills our happiness, but we neither know what our happiness is, nor the way. We are blind; left to ourselves we should take the wrong way; we must leave it to Him. Let us put ourselves into His hands, and not be startled though He leads us by a strange way, a *mirabilis via*, as the Church speaks. Let us be sure He will lead us right, that He will bring us to that which is, not indeed what we think best, nor what is best for another, but what is best for us.
>
> BLESSED JOHN HENRY NEWMAN

## We are members of God's household

So then you are no longer strangers and sojourners, but you are fellow citizens with the saints and members of the household of God, built upon the foundation of the apostles and prophets, Christ Jesus himself being the cornerstone, in whom the whole structure is joined together and grows into a holy temple in the Lord; in whom you also are built into it for a dwelling place of God in the Spirit.

EPHESIANS 2:19–22

*Silence*

*My petition for the day...*

Our Father...

**You give us others**

> The more we pray for someone, the more that blessing rests on him, for no prayer made in faith remains unanswered, even if the manner of its answering is hidden from us.
>
> SAINT GERTRUDE THE GREAT

Lord,
You give us others,
who watch, when we sleep,
who believe, when we doubt,
and keep praying,
when we are reduced to silence.

You give us others,
who walk with us,
who hope and fear with us,
who are tired and do not fail us,
to whom we can turn
with our cares and our needs.

You give us others,
who stand with us before you,
who ask you, and question,
and thank you,
and are always ready to serve you.

You give us others,
and entrust them to us.
We do not love you without them,
nor are we loved by you without them.
Let us be a blessing to one another,
on our way to you.
Amen.

May the Lord bless me, protect me from all evil,
and bring me to everlasting life.
+ In the name of the Father, and of the Son,
and of the Holy Spirit. Amen.

+ In the name of the Father, and of the Son,
and of the Holy Spirit. Amen.

*Quietly, I look back over this day. I call to mind the things and the people I have encountered in the course of this day and what I have thought, said, and done.*

Loving Father, I thank you for this day and for all the good things I have experienced. Forgive me, wherever I have sinned against you, against others, or against myself and let my heart rest in peace with you. Amen.

> To those wishing to practice interior prayer, especially to those who are beginners, I would counsel them to seek out the friendship and companionship of others who are also practicing meditation.
>
> SAINT TERESA OF AVILA

**Where two or three are gathered**

Lord, we ask you:
Be here in our midst
in this place of prayer –
and also at home in our village.
Lord, you have said:
Where two or three
are gathered in my name,
there I am among them.
Where two or three hear your word,
where two or three follow you,
where two or three – or many more –
wish to live your teachings, you are there too.
Lord, we trust in you,
we trust in your word.
Listen to our prayer,
be with us, stay with us!
Give us courage, and hope, and joy!
We ask this, O God, through Jesus Christ
Your Son, our Lord.
Amen.

From Zimbabwe

## Your face, Lord, do I seek

One thing have I asked of the LORD,
that will I seek after;
that I may dwell in the house of the LORD
all the days of my life,
to behold the beauty of the LORD,
and to inquire in his temple....
My heart says to you,
"Your face, LORD, do I seek."
Hide not your face from me....
I believe that I shall see the goodness of the LORD
in the land of the living!
Wait for the LORD;
be strong,
and let your heart take courage;
yes, wait for the LORD!
[Glory be to the Father, and to the Son,
and to the Holy Spirit,
as it was in the beginning, is now, and ever shall be,
world without end. Amen.]

PSALM 27:4, 8, 9, 13–14

> If you listen to Christ you will experience an ever greater joy in being a part of his Mystical Body, the Church, the family of his disciples, intimately joined in unity and love. Additionally, you will learn how to become reconciled with God, as the apostle Paul said.
>
> POPE BENEDICT XVI

## Stay with us, Lord

Stay with us, Lord Jesus, as evening falls; be our companion on our way. In your mercy inflame our hearts and raise our hope, so that, in union with our brethren, we may recognize you in the scriptures and in the breaking of Bread.
Who live and reign with the Father and the Holy Spirit, God, for ever and ever. Amen.

Prayer from Vespers of the Liturgy of the Hours

Lord, grant me a quiet night
and a perfect end in you.
+ In the name of the Father, and of the Son,
and of the Holy Spirit. Amen.

XC
Ἐγώ εἰμι
τὸ φῶς τοῦ
κόσμου
ὁ ἀκολου
θῶν ἐμοὶ
οὐ μὴ πε
ριπατήσῃ
ἐν τῇ σκο
τίᾳ ἀλλ' ἕ
ξει τὸ φῶς
τῆς ζωῆς

## SO THAT THE WORLD MAY BELIEVE – UNITY

+ In the name of the Father, and of the Son,
and of the Holy Spirit. Amen.

### In the silence of the dawn

Lord Jesus Christ,
in the silence of this new dawn I come to you and ask you with humble trust for your peace, your wisdom, your strength. Grant that I may contemplate the world today with eyes full of love. Help me to understand that all the glory of the Church springs from your Cross as its source. Let me welcome my neighbor as the person whom you wish to love through me. Grant me the willingness to serve him with devotion and to unfold all the goodness that you have placed within him.
Let my words radiate gentleness and my entire behavior be a source of peace. Let there dwell in my spirit only those thoughts that spread blessings. Stop up my ears to every malicious word and every ill-willed criticism. May my tongue serve only to highlight the good.
Grant above all, O Lord, that I may be so full of joy and goodwill that all who meet me will feel both your presence and your love.
Clothe me with the radiance of your goodness and your beauty, so that I may reveal you to others in the course of this day. Amen.

BLESSED MARIAM BAOUARDY

> Priority on the ecumenical path to unity should undoubtedly be given to prayer in common, to the mutual bond in prayer of all those who unite together around Christ himself. If Christians succeed, regardless of their divisions, to unite together more and more in common prayer around Christ, then their awareness will grow that what divides them, compared with what unites them, is small indeed.
>
> BLESSED JOHN PAUL II

**May they all be one**

[At that time Jesus prayed] "that they may all be one; even as you, Father, are in me, and I in you, that they also may be in us, so that the world may believe that you have sent me. The glory which you have given me I have given to them, that they may be one even as we are one, I in them and you in me, that they may become perfectly one, so that the world may know that you have sent me and have loved them even as you have loved me."

JOHN17:21–23

*Silence*

*My petition for the day...*

Our Father...

**We stand before you, Holy Spirit**

We stand before you, Holy Spirit,
Come to us, remain with us, and enlighten our hearts.
Give us light and strength to know your will,
to make it our own, and to live it in our lives.
Guide us by your wisdom, support us by your power,
do not allow us to be misled by ignorance
or corrupted by fear or favor.
Unite us to yourself in the bond of love
and keep us faithful to all that is true.
As we gather in your name, may we temper justice
with love, so that all our discussions and reflections
may be pleasing to you, and earn the reward promised
to good and faithful servants.
Amen.

Based on a prayer of the Vatican II Council Fathers, 1962

May the Lord bless me, protect me from all evil,
and bring me to everlasting life.
+ In the name of the Father, and of the Son,
and of the Holy Spirit. Amen.

+ In the name of the Father, and of the Son,
and of the Holy Spirit. Amen.

*Quietly, I look back over this day. I call to mind the things and the people I have encountered in the course of this day and what I have thought, said, and done.*

Loving Father, I thank you for this day and for all the good things I have experienced. Forgive me, wherever I have sinned against you, against others, or against myself and let my heart rest in peace with you. Amen.

> I therefore invite you, each day to seek the Lord, who desires nothing else than that you should be truly happy. Maintain a strong and lasting relationship with him in prayer and wherever possible organize moments in the course of your day in which you seek only his company.
>
> POPE BENEDICT XVI

**Into your loving care**

Into your loving care, dear Lord
We place our souls this night,
Keep us all safe within your heart
In peace till morning light.

And while our weary limbs find rest,
Keep our hearts fixed on you
For we are your trusting children too
Safe in your sheltering hand.

To Father, Son and Spirit blessed
We consecrate our sleep this night
And when the shades of death approach
Lead us to Heaven's eternal light.
Amen.

Liturgy of the Hours

**Never forget all his blessings**

Bless the LORD, O my soul;
and all that is within me, bless his holy name!
Bless the LORD, O my soul,
and forget not all his benefits,
who forgives all your iniquity,
who heals all your diseases,

In the Old Testament the eagle is an image of strength and endurance. The early Christians also saw the eagle as an image of the risen Lord, and also of every Christian, who in death is granted new life by God.

who redeems your life from the Pit,
who crowns you with mercy and compassion,
who satisfies you with good as long as you live
so that your youth is renewed like the eagle's.
The LORD works vindication and justice for all who are oppressed....
The LORD is merciful and gracious,
slow to anger and abounding in mercy....
Bless the LORD, O my soul!
[Glory be to the Father, and to the Son,
and to the Holy Spirit,
as it was in the beginning, is now, and ever shall be,
world without end. Amen.]

PSALM 103:1–6, 8, 22

**You were near, when I was far from you**

Jesus Christ, love of all love,
you were always with me,
and I knew it not.
You were there, and I forgot you.
You were deep in my heart,
and I sought you elsewhere.
Even when I was far from you,
you still waited for me.
The day is coming when I can say to you:
Risen Lord, you are my life.
To Christ I belong,
through Christ I exist.
Amen.

BROTHER ROGER SCHÜTZ

Lord, grant me a quiet night
and a perfect end in you.
+ In the name of the Father, and of the Son,
and of the Holy Spirit. Amen.

## YOU WILL TAKE OUT OUR HEARTS OF STONE – CONVERSION

+ In the name of the Father, and of the Son,
and of the Holy Spirit. Amen.

> We should always see both things – our weakness and our greatness. To be humble is to affirm and accept them both. We must hold ourselves in honor. In the end our humanity is an inexpressible mystery – entirely Godlike and entirely human. Inexpressibly beautiful and great. Man is the joy of God.
>
> ROMANO GUARDINI

### Help me to pray in the early morning

God, I call to you early in the morning.
Help me to pray
and to gather my thoughts to yourself,
for I cannot do it alone.
In me there is darkness, but in you there is light;
I am lonely, but you never leave me;
I am fainthearted, but in you is my help;
I am so restless, but in you there is peace;
in me there is bitterness, but there is patience in you;
I do not understand your ways,
but you know the way for me. Amen.

DIETRICH BONHOEFFER

### To seek and to save the lost

When Jesus came to the place, he looked up and said to him, "Zacchaeus, make haste and come down; for I must stay at your house today."... And when they saw it they all murmured, "He has gone in to be the guest of a man who is a sinner." And Zacchaeus stood and said to the Lord, "Behold, Lord, the half of my goods I give to the poor; and if I have defrauded any one of anything, I restore it fourfold." And Jesus said to him, "Today salvation has come to this house, since he also is a son of Abraham. For the Son of Man came to seek and to save the lost."

LUKE 19:7–10

> Anyone searching for something that is lost does not look in one place only but in many different places, here and there, for as long as it takes him to find it. See then, that is how God has to seek you, in all kinds of ways. Let him find you then, in every different way, in every turn of fate that befalls you, wherever it comes from, through whomever he chooses, in whatever belittlement, in whatever humiliation. See all these things as sent by God, for it is in such ways that he seeks you.
>
> JOHANNES TAULER

*Silence*

*My petition for the day...*

Our Father...

**Cut through my bonds**

My Jesus, I want to serve you, and cannot find the way.
I want to do good, and I cannot find the way.
I want to find you, and I cannot find the way.
I want to love you, and I cannot find the way.

I do not yet know you, my Jesus,
because I do not seek you.
I seek you, and I cannot find you.
Come to me, my Jesus.
I will never love you,
if you do not help me, my Jesus.
Cut through my bonds,
if you wish to have me.
Jesus, be Jesus to me. Amen.

SAINT PHILIP NERI

May the Lord bless me, protect me from all evil,
and bring me to everlasting life.
+ In the name of the Father, and of the Son,
and of the Holy Spirit. Amen.

+ In the name of the Father, and of the Son, and of the Holy Spirit. Amen.

*Quietly, I look back over this day. I call to mind the things and the people I have encountered in the course of this day and what I have thought, said, and done.*

Loving Father, I thank you for this day and for all the good things I have experienced. Forgive me, wherever I have sinned against you, against others, or against myself and let my heart rest in peace with you. Amen.

> ” Prayer always includes the fact that we must change our lives.
>
> ALFONS KIRCHGÄSSNER

**He loves you who has but strength to love**

Christ, divine Lord,
he loves you who has but strength to love:
unknowing, he who does not know you;
with longing, he who does.

Christ, you are my hope,
my peace, my happiness, all my life.
Christ, my spirit seeks you,
Christ, I adore you.

Christ, I cling to you
with all the power of my soul;
You, Lord, alone I love,
I seek you, I follow after you.
Amen.

ALPHANUS OF SALERNO

[A leper came to Jesus and said,] "Lord, if you will, you can make me clean."

MATTHEW 8:2, LUKE 5:12

## I will be your God

Thus says the Lord GOD:...
I will sprinkle clean water upon you,
and you shall be clean from all your uncleannesses,
and from all your idols I will cleanse you.
A new heart I will give you,
and a new spirit I will put within you;
and I will take out of your flesh the heart of stone
and give you a heart of flesh.
And I will put my spirit within you,
and cause you to walk in my statutes
and be careful to observe my ordinances.
You shall dwell in the land which I gave to your fathers;
and you shall be my people, and I will be your God.

EZEKIEL 36:25–28

## Dispel the darkness of this night

In your mercy, Lord,
dispel the darkness of this night.
Let your household so sleep in peace,
that at the dawn of a new day
they may, with joy, waken in your name.
Through Christ our Lord.
Amen.

Night prayer from the Liturgy of the Hours

Lord, grant me a quiet night
and a perfect end in you.
+ In the name of the Father, and of the Son,
and of the Holy Spirit. Amen.

THAT IS TODAY – EUCHARIST

+ In the name of the Father, and of the Son,
and of the Holy Spirit. Amen.

I am the bread of life. Your fathers ate the manna in the wilderness, and they died. This is the bread which comes down from heaven, that a man may eat of it and not die. I am the living bread which came down from heaven; if anyone eats of this bread, he will live for ever; and the bread which I shall give for the life of the world is my flesh.

JOHN 6:48–51

**Gather your Church together into your kingdom**

I thank you, Father, for the knowledge of Jesus and for letting me share my life with him. And I thank you for your Church, which proclaims his Gospel to me and through which he chooses to be with me, in his Word and Sacrament and in his mighty, yet silent presence in the world.
I pray for the Church, that it may be gathered together around your table.
For as the Bread of Life, which we eat, was once scattered as grain over the fields and then gathered again to become one loaf, so may your Church be gathered together from the ends of the earth and united as one in your kingdom.

Remember, Lord, your Church.
Deliver it from all evil and make it perfect in your love,
and gather it from the four winds into your kingdom.
[For yours is the power and the glory for ever. Amen.]

Based on the DIDACHE

**That is today**

On the day before he was to suffer for our salvation and the salvation of all, that is today, he took bread in his holy and venerable hands, and with eyes raised to heaven to you, O God, his almighty Father, giving you thanks, he said the blessing, broke the bread and gave it to his disciples, saying: take this, all of you and eat of it, for this is my body, which will be given up for you. In a similar way, when supper was ended, he took this precious chalice in his holy and venerable hands, and once more giving you thanks, he said the blessing and gave the chalice to his disciples, saying: take this, all of you and drink from it, for this is the chalice of my blood, the blood of the new and eternal covenant which will be poured out for you and for many for the forgiveness of sins. Do this in memory of me.

Eucharistic Prayer for Holy Thursday (based on MATTHEW 26:26–28 and 1 CORINTHIANS 11:23–25)

*Silence*

*My petition for the day...*

Our Father,

**Grow in me**

Grow, Jesus,
grow in me.
In my spirit,
in my heart,
in my imagination,
in my senses.
Grow in me in your gentleness,
in your purity,
in your humility,
your zeal, your love.
Grow in me with your grace,
your light and your peace.
Grow in me for the glorification of your Father,
for the greater honor of God.
Amen.

PIERRE OLIVAINT

May the Lord bless me, protect me from all evil,
and bring me to everlasting life.
+ In the name of the Father, and of the Son,
and of the Holy Spirit. Amen.

> In every Christian Christ lives his life, as it were, anew – first of all he is a child, then he grows to maturity until he reaches the age of the fully adult Christian. But he grows within in such a way that faith grows, love is strengthened and the Christian becomes ever more clearly aware of his Christian identity, and therefore lives his Christian life with ever greater depth and responsibility.
>
> ROMANO GUARDINI

+ In the name of the Father, and of the Son, and of the Holy Spirit. Amen.

*Quietly, I look back over this day. I call to mind the things and the people I have encountered in the course of this day and what I have thought, said, and done.*

Loving Father, I thank you for this day and for all the good things I have experienced. Forgive me, wherever I have sinned against you, against others, or against myself and let my heart rest in peace with you. Amen.

> Jesus, who died for the sins of all men, wishes to make a connection with each one of you and to knock at the door of your hearts in order to give you the gift of his grace. Meet him in the Blessed Eucharist, go into church to adore him, and kneel down before the Tabernacle. Then Jesus will fill you completely with his love and reveal to you the thoughts of his heart.
>
> POPE BENEDICT XVI

**You come to me, as I come to you**

Merciful Father,
You have sent us your Son.
He speaks to us through the words of Scripture.
He gives himself to us
under the forms of bread and wine.
It is you God, your very self, who come to me.
I come, like a sick man, to the doctor of life.
Unclean, to the fountain of mercy,
Blind, to the light of eternal brightness,
Poor and needy, to the Lord of heaven and earth.

Grant that I may not only outwardly
receive the sacrament
of the Body and Blood of Jesus,
but may also inwardly receive its grace and power,
and so be incorporated into his mystical Body.

Loving Father, in this life I receive your beloved Son
only under the outward veil of the sacrament.
Grant that I may one day look upon him, face to face,
unveiled and for all eternity.
Amen.

Based on a prayer by SAINT THOMAS AQUINAS

## Word in the Night

O taste and see that the LORD is good!
Blessed is the man who takes refuge in him!

PSALM 34:9

Humility consists in being precisely the person that you are before God, and since no two people are exactly identical, you will, provided you are sufficiently humble, be yourself, unlike anyone else in the world.

THOMAS MERTON

**The praises of God**

You are holy, Lord, the only God,
and your deeds are wonderful.
You are strong. You are great.
You are the most high.
You are the almighty King.
You, holy Father, are King of heaven and earth.
You are three and one,
Lord, God of gods.
You are good, all good, supreme good,
Lord, God, living and true
You are love.
You are wisdom.
You are humility.
You are patience.
You are beauty.
You are gentleness.
You are our protector.
You are rest.
You are peace.
You are joy and gladness.
You are justice and moderation.
You are all our riches and you suffice for us.
You are our guardian and defender.
You are our courage.
You are our haven and our hope.
...
You are our faith, our great consolation.
You are our eternal life,
great and wonderful Lord,
God Almighty, merciful Savior.
Amen.

SAINT FRANCIS OF ASSISI

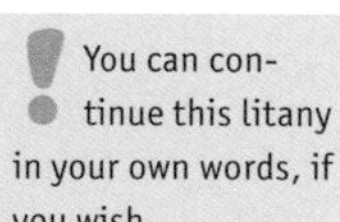

You can continue this litany in your own words, if you wish.

Lord, grant me a quiet night
and a perfect end in you.
+ In the name of the Father, and of the Son,
and of the Holy Spirit. Amen.

## GOD SHARES THE PAIN – THE PASSION OF CHRIST

+ In the name of the Father, and of the Son,
and of the Holy Spirit. Amen.

> For me, prayer is a surge of the heart; it is a simple look turned toward heaven, it is a cry of recognition and of love, embracing both trial and joy.
>
> SAINT THÉRÈSE OF LISIEUX

### Let me blindly walk your ways

Let me, Lord, blindly walk the way
that you present.
I understand not, but obey,
your child, content!
  Father of wisdom, and my Father too.
  Even by night, you lead me to you!
Lord, let it be just as you will,
I am ready to go!
Though my longing you may never fill,
in this world's woe.
  The When is for you – O Lord of all time.
  Your eternal Now will one day be mine!
May all that you plan come to pass as you will,
and wisely decree.
When you call me to sacrifice, silent and still,
Then give courage to me!
Amen.

SAINT TERESA BENEDICTA OF THE CROSS (EDITH STEIN)

## He became like us

Let each of you look not only to his own interests, but also to the interests of others. Have this mind among yourselves, which was in Christ Jesus, who, though he was in the form of God, did not count equality with God a thing to be grasped, but emptied himself, taking the form of a servant, being born in the likeness of men. And being found in human form he humbled himself and became obedient unto death, even death on a cross. Therefore God has highly exalted him and bestowed on him the name which is above every name, that at the name of Jesus every knee should bow, in heaven and on earth and under the earth, and every tongue confess that Jesus Christ is Lord, to the glory of God the Father.

PHILIPPIANS 2:4–11

*Silence*

*My petition for the day...*

Our Father...

## Lord, what do you want me to do?

Where should I go?
– Lead me there.
Who is this I am meeting?
– Show me the person.
What should I speak of, or not speak of?
– Show me what to do.
What do you want to do, my God?
Don't let me stand in your way.
Amen.

Based on the prayer of a fireman who died in the World Trade Center on September 11, 2001

May the Lord bless me, protect me from all evil,
and bring me to everlasting life.
+ In the name of the Father, and of the Son,
and of the Holy Spirit. Amen.

+ In the name of the Father, and of the Son,
and of the Holy Spirit. Amen.

*Quietly, I look back over this day. I call to mind the things and the people I have encountered in the course of this day and what I have thought, said, and done.*

Loving Father, I thank you for this day and for all the good things I have experienced. Forgive me, wherever I have sinned against you, against others, or against myself and let my heart rest in peace with you. Amen.

**Cross of Christ, that speaks of Easter**

Hail, Cross of Christ!
Wherever your mark is found,
Christ bears witness
to his Easter Mystery –
his passing from death to life.
He bears witness to love,
to the inner power of a life born of love
that overcomes death.
Hail, Cross of Christ!
Wherever you are raised up,
on the battlefields,
in the prison camps,
on the roadsides,
in all the places where people suffer
and struggle with death.
In the places where they work,
study and engage in creative activity.
In every place,
in the heart of every man and every woman,
every boy and every girl,
and in every human heart.
Hail, Cross of Christ! Amen.

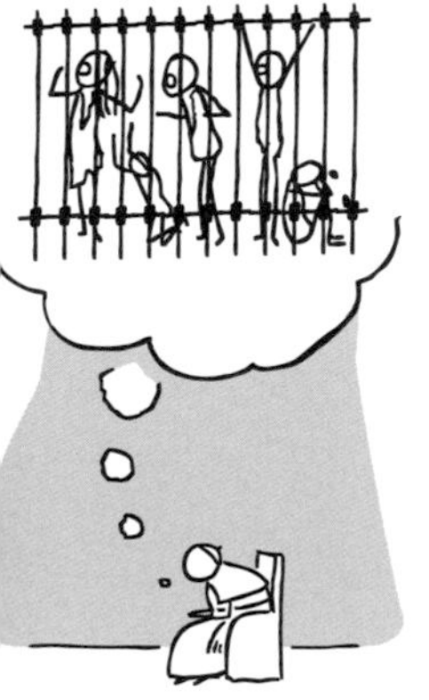

BLESSED JOHN PAUL II

**Why have you forsaken me?**

My God, my God, why have you forsaken me?
Why are you so far from helping me, from the words of my groaning?
O my God, I cry by day,
but you do not answer;
and by night, but find no rest.
Yet you are holy,
enthroned on the praises of Israel.
In you our fathers trusted;
they trusted, and you delivered them.
To you they cried, and were saved;
in you they trusted, and were not disappointed....
Be not far from me, for trouble is near
and there is none to help....
But you, O LORD, be not far off!
O my help, hasten to my aid!
[Glory be to the Father, and to the Son,
and to the Holy Spirit,
as it was in the beginning, is now, and ever shall be,
world without end. Amen.]

PSALM 22:1–5, 11, 19

The prayer of Christ reaches its high point on the Cross when he speaks the final words that the evangelists have recorded. At the point where he cries out in anguish, "My God, my God, why have you forsaken me?", Jesus in reality makes this plea the prayer of all those who are surrounded by enemies and have no one but God to whom they can turn.... And he brings this appeal before the heart of God. Hence, insofar as he is praying, in this final loneliness, together with the whole of humanity, he opens to us the heart of God.

POPE BENEDICT XVI

**No one – but you**

Sometimes, I feel like saying,
Just leave me all in peace!
Leave me alone! Go away!

I don't need you,
I don't want anyone to approach me,
I don't want anyone to give me advice,
I don't want anyone to decide for me,
I don't need anyone to live my life for me.

And yet, God,
I long for someone to be truly close,
I do need encouragement and advice,
I want and need understanding,
I thirst for true love.

You know all this,
Nothing is hidden from you.
For you I want to drop all my barriers,
I want to let you into my life,
I want you to be my King.

Thank you, God,
for still knocking at the door of my heart,
and not letting me be alone with myself.
Amen.

DÖRTE SCHRÖMGES

Lord, grant me a quiet night
and a perfect end in you.
+ In the name of the Father, and of the Son,
and of the Holy Spirit. Amen.

**FOR ALL ETERNITY – THE COVENANT WITH GOD**

+ In the name of the Father, and of the Son,
and of the Holy Spirit. Amen.

And God said [to Noah], "This is the sign of the covenant which I make between me and you and every living creature that is with you, for all future generations: I set my bow in the cloud, and it shall be a sign of the covenant between me and the earth."

GENESIS 9:12–13

**Praise at the dawn of the day**

In the rising light of dawn we praise you, O Lord,
for you are the Redeemer of all creation.
Grant us, in your mercy,
a day filled with your peace.

Forgive us our sins.
May our hope not falter.
Hide not your face from us.
You keep us in your caring love;
Do not weary of us.
You alone know our weakness.
Oh God, do not abandon us.
Amen.

From the East Syrian Church

## Benedictus

Blessed be the Lord God of Israel,
for he has visited and redeemed his people,
and has raised up a horn of salvation for us
in the house of his servant David,
as he spoke by the mouth of his holy prophets from of old,
that we should be saved from our enemies,
and from the hand of all who hate us;
to perform the mercy promised to our fathers,
and to remember his holy covenant,
the oath which he swore to our father Abraham,
to grant us
that we, being delivered from the hand of our enemies,
might serve him without fear,
in holiness and righteousness before him
all the days of our life.
And you, child, will be called the prophet
of the Most High;
for you will go before the Lord
to prepare his ways,
to give knowledge of salvation to his people
in the forgiveness of their sins,
through the tender mercy of our God,
when the day shall dawn upon us from on high
to give light to those who sit in darkness
and in the shadow of death,
to guide our feet into the way of peace.
[Glory be to the Father, and to the Son,
and to the Holy Spirit, as it was in the beginning,
is now, and ever shall be,
world without end. Amen.]

LUKE 1,68–79

The Benedictus is prayed by the Church every day at Morning Prayer (or Lauds, from the Latin word *laudes,* praise). It is a prophetic canticle, proclaimed by the priest Zechariah in Saint Luke's Gospel. Zechariah, the father of John the Baptist, does not believe the angel's message that his aged wife will conceive a son. So he is struck dumb for nine months. After his son is born and named by him, he is filled with the Holy Spirit and proclaims this inspired hymn in praise of the faithful and saving power of God in history, and the divine Redeemer who is about to come like the "dawn upon us from on high", and foretelling the life of his son, John, whom he calls a "prophet of the Most High".

*Silence*

*My petition for the day...*

Our Father...

### Sometimes, for a moment

Sometimes, for a moment,
I pause,
in the midst of the troubles of the day;
I close my eyes and ears,
and for a moment I am happy;
for I am not alone;
You are there, my God.
Amen.

### Aaron's Blessing

Lord, bless me and keep me; let your face shine upon me and be gracious to me. Lift up your countenance upon me and give me peace.
+ In the name of the Father, and of the Son,
and of the Holy Spirit. Amen.

Based on NUMBERS 6:24–26

+ In the name of the Father, and of the Son, and of the Holy Spirit. Amen.

*Quietly, I look back over this day. I call to mind the things and the people I have encountered in the course of this day and what I have thought, said, and done.*

Loving Father, I thank you for this day and for all the good things I have experienced. Forgive me, wherever I have sinned against you, against others, or against myself and let my heart rest in peace with you. Amen.

**God by whose Word the world was made**

God by whose Word the world was made,
and by whose will it moves,
you clothe the day in heavenly light
and bless our sleep by night.

So fill our hearts with dreams of you,
as peace enfolds us now.
May tranquil sleep refresh our souls
to rise with strength renewed.

All praise to God the Father be,
to Son and Spirit blest,
the Triune God who all things moves.
Save us, who trust in thee. Amen.

SAINT AMBROSE OF MILAN

As my prayer became ever more contemplative and interior, I found I had less and less to say. Finally I became completely silent. I became what is, if possible, an even greater contrast to speaking: I became a listener. At first I thought that prayer was speaking, but then I learned that prayer is not merely silence, but listening.
It is like this then: prayer means not hearing oneself speak. Prayer means becoming silent and being silent and waiting, until the person praying hears God.

SØREN KIERKEGAARD

**He who keeps you will not slumber**

I lift up my eyes to the hills.
From where does my help come?
My help comes from the LORD,
who made heaven and earth.
He will not let your foot be moved,
he who keeps you will not slumber.
Behold, he who keeps Israel
will neither slumber nor sleep.
The LORD is your keeper;
the LORD is your shade
on your right hand.
The sun shall not strike you by day,
nor the moon by night.
The LORD will keep you from all evil;
he will keep your life.
The LORD will keep
your going out and your coming in
from this time forth and for evermore.
[Glory be to the Father, and to the Son,
and to the Holy Spirit,
as it was in the beginning, is now, and ever shall be,
world without end. Amen.]

PSALM 121

> If we were to limit ourselves to reciting old prayers, we would not feel impelled to express the newness of God in a new way. And so, it is to be feared, we might begin to pigeonhole God in our lives, in our understanding. But then he would no longer be the true God, and we would ultimately perhaps be praying no longer to him, the Living One, but to ourselves, the dead ones.
>
> HEINRICH SPAEMANN

### Through water to you

Faithful God,
just as the Israelites passed through water
from slavery to freedom,
so I once passed through the waters of baptism
and now belong to you.
Just as you once sealed
an indissoluble covenant with your people,
so you have indissolubly bound yourself to me.

Remind me, Lord,
so that I may never forget your faithfulness.
Renew your covenant within me so that,
united with you, I may live
in the new land you are giving us,
may find the new freedom you promise us,
and may live the new life that death cannot kill.
Amen.

GEORG LENGERKE

Lord, grant me a quiet night
and a perfect end in you.
+ In the name of the Father, and of the Son,
and of the Holy Spirit. Amen.

# PART TWO

# 2 You have called us friends

**MY LIFE, IN PRAYER**

# Praising the Father

## Our Father

Our Father who art in heaven,
Hallowed be thy name.
Thy kingdom come,
Thy will be done
On earth as it is in heaven.
Give us this day our daily bread;
And forgive us our trespasses
As we forgive those who trespass against us;
And lead us not into temptation,
But deliver us from evil.
[For thine is the kingdom and the power
and the glory for ever and ever.
Amen.]

MATTHEW 6:9–13

He [Jesus] was praying in a certain place, and when he ceased, one of his disciples said to him, "Lord, teach us to pray, as John taught his disciples." And he said to them, "When you pray, say: 'Father, hallowed be your name....'"

LUKE 11:1–2

## Credo – I believe (Apostles' Creed)

I believe in God,
the Father almighty,
Creator of heaven and earth,
and in Jesus Christ, his only Son, our Lord,
who was conceived by the Holy Spirit,
born of the Virgin Mary,
suffered under Pontius Pilate,
was crucified, died and was buried;
he descended into hell;
on the third day he rose again from the dead;
he ascended into heaven,
and is seated at the right hand of God the Father almighty;
from there he will come to judge the living and the dead.
I believe in the Holy Spirit,
the holy catholic Church,

the communion of saints,
the forgiveness of sins,
the resurrection of the body,
and life everlasting. Amen.

> But what is the point of the old, traditionally formulated prayers? What claim do they still have? They are a sharing in people's experiences of God and their encounters with God over the millennia. They are our bond of fellowship with countless prayerful souls who understand that they come from God and live lives directed toward him. They are the memory of an unending chain of God's promptings and providence throughout the history of the People of God, and they preserve us from the disastrous consequences of forgetting the Covenant with God – without which we are not sons of God.
>
> HEINRICH SPAEMANN

## Gloria – Glory to God

Glory to God in the highest,
and on earth peace to people of good will.
We praise you,
we bless you,
we adore you,
we glorify you,
we give you thanks for your great glory,
Lord God, heavenly King,
O God, almighty Father.
Lord Jesus Christ, Only Begotten Son,
Lord God, Lamb of God, Son of the Father,
you take away the sins of the world,
have mercy on us;
you take away the sins of the world,
receive our prayer;
you are seated at the right hand of the Father,
have mercy on us.
For you alone are the Holy One,
you alone are the Lord,
you alone are the Most High,
Jesus Christ,
with the Holy Spirit,
in the glory of God the Father.
Amen.

From the Liturgy of the Church, ninth century

## Sanctus – Holy, Holy, Holy

Holy, Holy, Holy
Lord God of hosts.
Heaven and earth are full of your glory.
Hosanna in the highest.
Blessed is he who comes in the name of the Lord.
Hosanna in the highest.

From the Liturgy of the Eucharist (see ISAIAH 6:3 and PSALM 118:26)

## Te Deum – We praise you, O God

We praise you, O God: we acclaim you as the Lord.
Everlasting Father, all the world bows down before you.
All the angels sing praise, the hosts of heaven and all the angelic powers,
all the cherubim and seraphim call out to you in unending song:
Holy, Holy, Holy is the Lord God of angel hosts!
The heavens and the earth are filled with your majesty and glory.

The glorious band of apostles, the noble company of prophets,
the white-robed army who shed their blood for Christ,
all sing your praise.
And to the ends of the earth your holy Church proclaims her faith in you:
Father, whose majesty is boundless,
your true and only Son, who is to be adored,
the Holy Spirit sent to be our Advocate.

You, Christ are the king of glory,
Son of the eternal Father.
When you took our nature to save mankind
you did not shrink
from birth in the Virgin's womb.
You overcame the power of death,
opening the Father's kingdom
to all who believe in you.

* We praise you, God! – ** We acclaim you as the Lord!

Enthroned at God's right hand
in the glory of the Father,
you will come in judgment
according to your promise.
You redeemed your people by your precious blood.
Come, we implore you, to our aid.
Grant us with the saints a place in eternal glory.
Amen.

The Te Deum is also known as the Ambrosian Hymn. According to an ancient tradition it arose spontaneously during the Easter Vigil liturgy in the year 387. As the holy Bishop Ambrose of Milan was baptizing the newly converted Augustine, the future saint, seized by the Holy Spirit, began to sing spontaneously – while his baptizer, Saint Ambrose, responded, verse for verse.

## Magnificat

My soul magnifies the Lord,
and my spirit rejoices in God my Savior,
for he has regarded the low estate of his handmaiden.
For behold, henceforth all generations will call me blessed;
for he who is mighty has done great things for me,
and holy is his name.
And his mercy is on those who fear him
from generation to generation.
He has shown strength with his arm,
he has scattered the proud in the imagination of their hearts,
he has put down the mighty from their thrones,
and exalted those of low degree;
he has filled the hungry with good things,
and the rich he has sent empty away.
He has helped his servant Israel,
in remembrance of his mercy,
as he spoke to our fathers,
to Abraham and to his posterity for ever.
[Glory be to the Father, and to the Son,
and to the Holy Spirit, as it was in the beginning,
is now, and ever shall be,
world without end. Amen.]

LUKE 1:46–55

**How deep is your wisdom**

O my God,
how deep is your wisdom,
how unsearchable your judgments,
how inscrutable your ways!
For who has ever known your thoughts, O Lord?
Or who has been your counselor?
Who has ever given you anything,
so that you had to repay him?
From you everything has its beginning,
through you everything has life,
in you everything has its goal.
All that I have, I have from you.
All that I am, is determined by you.
To you be all honor and praise,
now and for all eternity. Amen.

Based on ROMANS 11:33–36

**All from your loving hands**

From nearest field, to distant lands,
Everything comes from your loving hands:
the corn stalk and the distant star,
the grain of sand, the ocean far.
From you come leaf and bush and blade,
from you come fruit and corn;
the gentle sunshine in the spring,
the snow and hail and storm.
You make the sun to rise each day,

you guide the moon's fair course;
you cause the winds to rise and blow
and send clouds swiftly past.
You make our hearts to glow with joy,
our faces fresh and red,
you feed the cows on meadow hay
and give your children bread.
Amen.

Based on a poem by MATTHIAS CLAUDIUS

**The eyes of all look to you**

Lord, you are gracious and merciful,
slow to anger and abounding in mercy.
You are good to all,
and your compassion is over all that you have made.
You uphold all who fall,
and raise up all who are bowed down.
The eyes of all look to you,
and you give them their food in due season.
You open your hand,
you satisfy the desire of every living thing.
[Glory be to the Father, and to the Son,
and to the Holy Spirit, as it was in the beginning,
is now, and ever shall be,
world without end. Amen.]

Based on PSALM 145

**O God, creation's secret force**

O God, creation's secret force,
yourself unmoved, all motion's source,
who from morn till evening ray
through all its changes guide the day:

Grant us, when this short life is past,
The glorious evening that shall last;
That by a holy death attained,
Eternal glory may be gained.

Attributed to SAINT AMBROSE OF MILAN

# Listening to the Son

## You are God the Son

Lord, you look at me,
and I look at you.
You are the living Word of the Father,
through whom he created the world.
And you have become man, just like I am.
You are the Son of God and the Son of the Virgin Mary,
who said Yes to your coming into the world.
You are the Good Shepherd who seeks out the lost sheep.
You are the vine and we are the branches.
You are the door to the Father, and the Father's door to me.
You are God's sympathy and shared joy in us.
You are God's pardon for our sins,
and his mercy on us.
You are the grain of wheat that was ground and made bread
and which gives us life.
You are the image of God, in whom we see the Father.
You are his Love incarnate, which will never abandon me
and which is stronger than death.
You are the Resurrection and the Life for all
who trust in you, who believe in you and follow you.
You are the just Judge, who will one day return,
upholding the outcast and redeeming our lives.
And one day you will be all in all for me.
I will look on you and you on me.
I will see you as you are
and rejoice in you,
with all who belong to you,
for all eternity.
Amen.

DÖRTE SCHRÖMGES / GEORG LENGERKE

You are the Christ, the Son of the Living God.

Saint Peter, in MATTHEW 16:16

### Lord, make your home in me

Come, Lord, so that Christmas can come
to the house of my life.
So many have lived in it,
while there was no place for you.
I have opened the door to guests
who soiled it and despoiled it.
And sometimes I lost all joy in living
in the house of my own life.
So please, make your home now, in these empty rooms;
fill my house with Light and Presence
and go even into every last
forgotten, guilt-filled chamber.
Come in, with the wonder of your Peace,
and stay with me forever.
Amen.

BERNHARD MEUSER

### Jesus, you are in my heart

Jesus, you are in my heart,
I believe in your love for me,
and I love you. Amen.

BLESSED TERESA OF CALCUTTA

### Teach me, Lord, day by day

I need Thee to teach me day by day,
according to each day's opportunities and needs.
Give me, O my Lord, that purity of conscience
which alone can receive Thy inspirations.

My ears are dull, so that I cannot hear Thy voice.
My eyes are dim, so that I cannot see Thy tokens.

Thou alone canst quicken my hearing, and purge my sight,
and cleanse and renew my heart.
Teach me to sit at Thy feet, and to hear Thy word. Amen.

BLESSED JOHN HENRY NEWMAN

**Merciful Jesus, I trust in you!**

Merciful Jesus, I trust in you!
Let nothing alarm or disturb me anymore.

I trust in you, morning and evening, in joy and in suffering,
in temptations and dangers, in happiness and misfortune,
in life and death, for time and eternity.
I trust in you, in prayer and at my work,
in success and failure, in waking and in resting,
in trouble and sadness –
yes, even in my failings and sins
I resolve to trust unshakably in you.

You are the anchorage of my hope,
the guiding star of my wanderings,
the support of my weakness,
the forgiveness of my sins,
the strength of my virtues,
the fulfillment of my life,
the consolation of my dying hour,
the joy and bliss of my heaven.

Merciful Jesus, strong rest and sure fortress of my soul,
increase my trust and perfect my faith
in your power and goodness.
Though I am the poorest of your adorers and the least of your servants,
yet I wish to be great and perfect in trust
that you are my salvation and my redemption for all eternity.

May this, my trust, recommend me to you,
now and for all time – but most of all at the hour of my death!
Amen.

SAINT FAUSTINA KOWALSKA





Many people err in imagining that many different things, many different methods are needed in order to make prayer good. I do not say that one should not make use of particular methods; but we should not cling to them or hang on to them to the extent that we put all our trust in them. In order to pray well, one thing only is necessary, namely, to hold our Lord in our arms. When we do this, our prayer is always well made, no matter in what way we may choose to approach it.

SAINT FRANCIS DE SALES

**O holy cross of hope**

O most holy Cross,
on which my Lord did hang,
in deathly fear and pain.

See how with spear and nails,
his every limb is torn,
Pierced are his hands and feet
and side.

You are the sturdy Ladder,
on which we climb to Life,
Life that God gives forever.

You are the solid Bridge,
by which your faithful children
cross safe over the raging tide.

INRI

You are the victorious Sign,
before whom Satan shrinks,
fear-struck at the very sight.

You are the pilgrim's Staff,
on which we can safely lean,
not wavering, not falling.

How can we duly praise you,
in whom all good is found
that ever was poured out on us.

> Jesus, for you I live; Jesus, for you I die; Jesus, I am yours in life and in death.
>
> Church chant, Augsburg, Germany 1667

You are the Key of Heaven,
opening the door to the Life
that first you gained for us.

Show now your strength
and power,
shield and protect us all,
through your holy Name, O
Lord.

So may we die in peace,
as children of our God,
heirs to the Father's Kingdom.

Traditional German hymn, circa 1600

**Lord, send us**

Lord, send us.
Whenever you will it,
let us leave the house behind us
that has grown dear to us,
that was our place of prayer, of doubt, of adoration,
that was for us the stone upon which we had settled,
that was the space that knew us,
the place that sheltered us.

Whenever you will it,
let us leave behind the brothers and sisters whom we know,
whom we have loved, angered, blessed,
the saints and sinners and the middling ones
with whom for decades we have believed and prayed,
worked and sweated,
eaten and drunk together under one roof.

Whenever you will it,
we will take leave
of the hands and prayers that bore us,
of the eyes that called to us,
of the house we helped to build,
that has now become a part of us.

Whenever you will it,
we will bid farewell.
For you are calling us.
You are sending us.

And wherever we settle, you are there already.
You who have borne us, molded, guided, freed us; you are there already.
You who lead us in new and unimagined ways, you are there already.
We walk with you, encounter you, in ways we could never have believed –
for you are already there.

We set out,
and we are not abandoned –
for you go with us.
Amen.

Based on a homily of SAINT BERNARD OF CLAIRVAUX

# Invoking the Holy Spirit

**Come, Holy Spirit**

Come, Holy Spirit,
send forth the heavenly
radiance of your light.

Come, father of the poor,
come giver of gifts,
come, light of the heart.

Greatest comforter,
sweet guest of the soul,
sweet consolation.

In labor, rest,
in heat, temperance,
in tears, solace.

O most blessed light,
fill the inmost heart
of your faithful.

Without your grace,
there is nothing in us,
nothing that is not harmful.

For you did not receive the spirit of slavery to fall back into fear, but you have received the spirit of sonship. When we cry, "Abba! Father!" it is the Spirit himself bearing witness with our spirit that we are children of God.

Saint Paul, in his letter to the ROMANS 8:15–16

Likewise the Spirit helps us in our weakness; for we do not know how to pray as we ought, but the Spirit himself intercedes for us with sighs too deep for words.

ROMANS 8:26

Cleanse that which is unclean,
water that which is dry,
heal that which is wounded.

Bend that which is inflexible,
fire that which is chilled,
correct what goes astray.

Give to your faithful,
those who trust in you,
the sevenfold gifts.

Grant the reward of virtue,
grant the deliverance of salvation,
grant eternal joy.

STEPHEN LANGTON, Archbishop of Canterbury (d. 1228)

> Prayer is a gift of the Holy Spirit, that makes us into men and women of hope, and prayer enables us to keep the world open for God.
>
> POPE BENEDICT XVI

**Breathe in me, O Holy Spirit**

Breathe in me, O Holy Spirit,
that my thoughts may all be holy.
Act in me, O Holy Spirit,
that my work, too, may be holy.
Draw my heart, O Holy Spirit,
that I may love but what is holy.
Strengthen me, O Holy Spirit,
to defend all that is holy.
Guard me, then, O Holy Spirit,
that I always may be holy.
Amen.

SAINT AUGUSTINE OF HIPPO

## Come, Creator Spirit

Come, Holy Ghost, Creator, come
From thy bright heavenly throne,
Come, take possession of our souls,
And make them all thine own.

Thou who art called the Paraclete,
Best gift of God above,
The living spring, the living fire,
Sweet unction and true love.

Thou who art sevenfold in thy grace,
Finger of God's right hand;
His promise, teaching little ones
To speak and understand.

O guide our minds with thy blest light,
With love our hearts inflame;
And with thy strength, which ne'er decays,
Confirm our mortal frame.

Far from us drive our deadly foe;
True peace unto us bring;
And through all perils lead us safe
Beneath thy sacred wing.

Through thee may we the Father know,
Through th' eternal Son,
And thee the Spirit of them both,
Thrice-blessed Three in One.

All glory to the Father be,
With his co-equal Son:
The same to thee, great Paraclete,
While endless ages run.

BLESSED RABANUS MAURUS

> One thing indeed is necessary: that we should hunger for the good Spirit, should need him still more urgently than a child needs bread, fish and eggs in order to live this earthly life. And that, in such hunger, we should beg God for this Spirit!
>
> HEINRICH SPAEMANN

What distinguishes the prayer of Christians from that of others who pray is this: God comes to us in our humanity, without leaving heaven; God himself wants to lead us to him. Prayer means being drawn into the relationship that already exists in God. Prayer means taking part in the eternal conversation between the Father and the Son in the Holy Spirit.

## You create and penetrate all things

All things you penetrate,
the heights, the depths
and every abyss.
You build and bind all things.
Through you the clouds file past,
the air steering their sails.
Through you the hard rock brings forth water,
the rivulets run,
and from the earth the fresh green wells up.
Far afield, you also lead
the Spirit,
who drinks of your teachings.
You breathe wisdom into him,
and with the wisdom, joy.
Amen.

SAINT HILDEGARD OF BINGEN

## Soul of my soul

O Holy Spirit, Soul of my soul,
Humbly I adore You.

Enlighten, guide, strengthen and console me.
Unveil your wishes to me,
so far as this lies in the plan of God the eternal Father.
Tell me what eternal Love desires of me.
Tell me what I ought to do.
Tell me what I must suffer.
Tell me what I must accept, bear and endure.

Yes, Holy Spirit, let me know your will
and the will of the Father.
For henceforth my whole life seeks nothing but to be
a permanent, everlasting yes to the will of God the eternal Father.
Amen.

FATHER JOSEF KENTENICH based on a prayer by Cardinal Mercier

**Unusual invocations to the Holy Spirit**

Holy Spirit – source of truth,
Breath of God – giver of life!

| | |
|---|---|
| Surprise me | in the midst of daily life. |
| Go with me | even into my plans. |
| Transform me | in my understanding. |
| Fill me | with all your gifts. |
| Immerse me | to make me clean. |
| Awaken my talents | to work in me. |
| Work in me | that I may grow less. |
| Ignite your charism | that I may witness to you. |
| Overtake me | when I flee. |
| Gather me up | when I wander aimlessly. |
| Urge me on | when I start to flag. |
| Give me wings | when I work creatively. |
| Hasten to me | when I seek you. |
| Walk beside me | when I am pensive. |
| Enlighten me | when I do not understand. |
| Break me open | when I freeze |
| Pour into me | when I am hesitant |
| Purify me | when I am tempted |
| Burn within me | when I grow cold |
| Overwhelm me | when I become complacent |
| Flood through me | when I am empty |
| Fill me with joy | when I am sad |
| Embrace me | when I am lonely |
| Pray in me | when I cannot find the words |
| Console me | when I am abandoned |
| Heal me | when I am sick |
| Hold me | when I fall |
| Shelter me | when I am defenseless |
| Seize me | when I burn with longing |
| Rejoice in me | when I love you |

# Adoring God

## Praying the Sign of the Cross

In the name of the Father,
who created us
and loves us
and will not let us be lost in eternity,
And of the Son,
In whom God gives himself,
in my life and in my body,
in the world and its sufferings, even down to the underworld,
And of the Holy Spirit
who unites them both and consoles and guides us
and binds us together with one another and with HIM,
in the power of his Resurrection.

Enlighten my spirit,
my thoughts,
my reason and my understanding,
and brighten my gaze,
Fill my body
With your holy presence,
awaken in it the power of your creation
and of the Holy Spirit, whose dwelling it is.
Guide my hands,
to make them free
for the hand that you reach out,
and for the work you give me to do.

Then all that I am and have,
all that I do and long for,
may be directed to you and with you –
for your glory and the salvation of our humanity.
Amen.

GEORG LENGERKE

The Sign of the Cross signifies both the Cross and our own bodies. In Jesus, God took this body fully to himself. It then signifies (from top to bottom) the movement of God, in his Son, down to us, and (from left to right) the binding and driving, consoling and reminding power of the Holy Spirit through world time. Finally, it is the plea for the blessing and the light of God on our own spirits, our hearts, and our hands, on all that we think, feel, and do.

**The journey within**

I sit here before you, Lord,
upright and relaxed, my spine straight.
I let my weight sink down, vertically, through my body
onto the floor on which I am sitting.

I keep my spirit firmly within my body.
I resist its urge to escape
out of the window,
to be in any other place but this one here,
to escape into the time before and after,
to avoid the present.
Gently and firmly, I hold my spirit there,
where my body is,
here in this room.

In this present moment
I let go of all my plans, concerns and fears.
I lay them now in your hands, Lord,
I relax the grip in which I hold them and leave them to you.
For the moment, I leave them to you.
I wait for you – expectantly.
You come to me, and I let myself be carried by you.

I begin the journey within.
I travel into myself, to the innermost core of my being,
where you live.
At this deepest point of my being
you are always there already, waiting for me,
ceaselessly creating, enlivening, strengthening my whole person.

And now I open my eyes,
to look at you in the world of things
and people.
With new strength I go into life,
no longer alone,
but together with my Creator.
Amen.

DAG HAMMARSKJÖLD

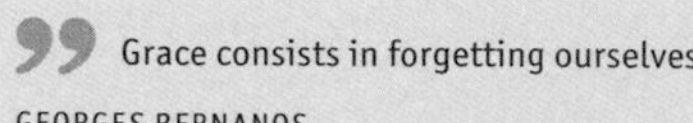

Grace consists in forgetting ourselves.

GEORGES BERNANOS

## I abandon myself into your hands

Father,
I abandon myself into your hands;
do with me what you will.
Whatever you may do, I thank you:
I am ready for all, I accept all.
Let only your will be done in me,
and in all your creatures –
I wish no more than this, O Lord.
Into your hands I commend my soul:
I offer it to you
with all the love of my heart,
for I love you, Lord,
and so need to give myself,
to surrender myself into your hands without reserve,
and with boundless confidence,
for you are my Father.
Amen.

BLESSED CHARLES DE FOUCAULD

> And now entrust everything to him. He is the Father. His providence embraces all things. Not one hair falls from our head but he knows the reason. Do not doubt his wisdom. God's guidance is beyond our understanding. Simply trust in him, without reserve.
>
> ROMANO GUARDINI

## May I become what you give me

Lord, you are the Bread of life.
You give your very self to me.
And in this Eucharistic bread
I receive what I am – the Body of Christ,
so that I may become what I receive –
the Body of Christ.
Amen.

Based on a sermon by SAINT AUGUSTINE OF HIPPO

> Now you are the body of Christ and individually members of it.
>
> 1 CORINTHIANS 12:27

> Look upon Jesus in the Tabernacle. Fix your eyes on him, who is the Light; come with your hearts close to his divine Heart; beg him for the grace to recognize him, for a heart to love him, the courage to serve him. Seek him passionately. Every moment in prayer – especially before our Lord in the Tabernacle – is a certain gain.
>
> BLESSED TERESA OF CALCUTTA

## Godhead here in hiding

Godhead here in hiding, whom I do adore,
Masked by these bare shadows, shape and nothing more,
See, Lord, at thy service low lies here a heart
Lost, all lost in wonder at the God thou art.

Seeing, touching, tasting are in thee deceived;
How says trusty hearing? that shall be believed;
What God's Son has told me, take for truth I do;
Truth himself speaks truly or there's nothing true.

On the cross thy Godhead made no sign to men;
Here thy very manhood steals from human ken:
Both are my confession, both are my belief,
And I pray the prayer of the dying thief.

I am not like Thomas, wounds I cannot see,
But I plainly call thee Lord and God as he:
This faith each day deeper be my holding of,
Daily make me harder hope and dearer love.

O Thou, our reminder of the Crucified,
Living Bread, the life of us for whom he died,
Lend this life to me, then; feed and feast my mind,
There be thou the sweetness man was meant to find.

Like what tender tales tell of the Pelican,
Bathe me, Jesus Lord, in what thy bosom ran
Blood that but one drop of has the power to win
All the world forgiveness of its world of sin.

Jesus, whom I look at shrouded here below,
I beseech thee, send me what I thirst for so,
Some day to gaze on thee face to face in light
And be blest forever with thy glory's sight.
Amen.

SAINT THOMAS AQUINAS

JOHN 20:19–29

In ancient mythology the pelican is portrayed as pecking its own breast in order to feed its starving young and revive them with its own blood. This image was taken up by the early Christians as a metaphor for the passion of Christ and the holy Eucharist, and so found its way into Christian art.

## Don't let me lose my way

I do not know
who you are,
I do not know
What you are like,
I do not know
where you are.

But I do know, O God,
that I lose
my own way
if I do not seek you.
Amen.

BERNHARD MEUSER

> The diligent soul will find a place of prayer everywhere, for she constantly carries it within herself.
>
> SAINT CATHERINE OF SIENA



## Not without your love

I love you, my God,
and my only wish is to love you
until the last moment of my life.
I love you, O my infinitely lovable God,
and I would rather die in your love
than live even for a single moment longer without it.
I love you, Lord,
and the only grace I ask of you
is to be permitted to love you eternally.
My God, if my lips cannot tell you every moment
that I love you,
then I desire that my heart may repeat it
with every beat.
Amen.

SAINT JEAN-MARIE VIANNEY, THE CURÉ OF ARS

> The progress of the soul consists not in thinking a great deal about God, but in loving God greatly; and one acquires this love when one determines to do a great deal for him.
>
> SAINT TERESA OF AVILA

# Accepting forgiveness and redemption

## Confiteor – I confess

I confess to almighty God,
To you, who alone know my heart and my history,
who alone can forgive sins,
who alone can take from me
my heavy burden
and restore what I have spoiled;
and to you, my brothers and sisters,
to those against whom I have trespassed,
to those who have trespassed against me
and to those who, like me, are sinners
and with me call out to you;
that I have greatly sinned, in my thoughts and in my words,
in what I have done:
the evil I let myself be led astray into doing,
because it seemed so plausible;
and in what I have failed to do:
the good that you offered me and that I rejected;
through my fault,
which cannot be glossed over,
through my fault,
which I fully acknowledge,
through my most grievous fault,
which separates me from you – and from myself.
Therefore I ask blessed Mary ever-Virgin,
all the Angels and Saints,
and all the Church Triumphant, already in heaven
and interceding for us,
and you, my brothers and sisters,
to whom I no longer try to pretend,
who now know that I seek forgiveness and forbearance
and with whom I stand before God

to pray for me to the Lord our God,
that you, O God, may show me your merciful gaze
on my life and that of my brothers and sisters,
that I may throw myself in your arms, with all that I have done and suffered,
and that you may forgive me
my sins against you, against others
and against my own soul.
Amen.

GEORG LENGERKE, a prayer based on the Confiteor *(I Confess)*

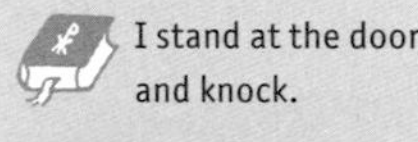

I stand at the door and knock.

REVELATION 3:20

The thrice repeated striking of the breast during the Confiteor in Holy Mass is like God knocking at the door. We may ask ourselves, What? At the very moment when I remember that my soul looks like a pigsty within? Now, of all times, he knocks and wants to come in? There is no time left; there is nothing more I can do to clean up, nothing more to put things right myself. So I let him in, to everything that is inside me and is a part of me. He comes – and wherever he is admitted, everything is put right again.

## Who is a God like you?

Who is a God like you,
pardoning my iniquity
and forgiving the transgressions of your people?
You do not forever remain angry with me
for the sins I have committed against you.
For you delight in mercy.
You will again have compassion on me,
and tread my iniquities under foot.
Yes, you will cast all my sins
into the depths of the sea.
You will show faithfulness to your children,
and your mercy to us, just as you promised
to those who believed in you,
from the days of old until this day.
Amen.

based on MICAH 7:18–20

We have escaped as a bird from the snare of the fowlers; the snare is broken, and we have escaped! Our help is in the name of the LORD, who made heaven and earth.

PSALM 124:7–8

## Freed from idols

Praise to you, my God,
for having freed me from idols.
You have given me the grace to praise only you
and not the manufactured gods
or technology
or justice
or the need to please
or humanism
or progress
or anyone in particular
or tolerance
or sex
or being beautiful
or consumerism
or networking
or a brand name
or intoxication
or science
or the Internet
or flat rate charges
or profit
...
You redeem me from ideologies
that only explain themselves,
and clever notions
that are merely thought up,
and the virtual world
that takes itself for reality.
I know that you are God, not of the dead,
but of the living.
Praise to you, my God,
who have freed me from death!
Amen.

Inspired by an idea of PAUL CLAUDEL

> ! You can also use this prayer in preparation for confession. You can extend the list by adding the big and powerful attractions that seek to take the place of God for you.

**Forgive me**

Lord, help me to recognize
where I am at fault,
where I misuse power
and will not acknowledge wrongdoing;
where I am silent,
keep my mouth shut,
look the other way.
Forgive me my sins. Amen.

> By humble and faithful prayer, the soul acquires, with time and perseverance, every virtue.
>
> SIMONE WEIL

**My Lord and my God**

My Lord and my God,
take from me everything that distances me from you.
My Lord and my God,
give me everything that brings me closer to you.
My Lord and my God,
detach me from myself to give my all to you.
Amen.

SAINT NICHOLAS OF FLÜE

**You heal the gaping rifts**

Christ, you accept us with our heart
just as it is today.
Why should we wait, then,
for our heart to change
before we come to you?
You change it each day anew,
without our knowing how.
You do everything
to heal the gaping rifts –
You, our friend and brother Jesus Christ.
Amen.

BROTHER ROGER SCHÜTZ

In every human being there is a stratum of solitude that no human affection can entirely fill, not even the most powerful love between two people. Whoever will not consent to enter this place of solitude is living in rebellion, in rebellion against mankind and even against God. It is there in the depths of your being, where no individual is like another, that Christ awaits you.

From the Rule of Taizé

### On the road of life

Let us pray
for all those who are travelling
on the road of life:
for the proud, the arrogant, the self-righteous
   and for all that is proud, arrogant,
   and self-righteous within us;
for the weary, the tired of life, the resigned,
   and for all that is weary, tired of life,
   and resigned within us;
for the well-fed, blinded by consumerism and self-satisfied,
   and for all that is well-fed, blind,
   and self-satisfied within us;
for the angry, the violent and the vengeful,
   and for all that is angry, violent,
   and vengeful within us;
for the loveless, for those who in their love seek only themselves,
   and for all that is loveless
   and self-seeking within us;
for the envious, the ill-willed, who see in others only rivals,
   and for all within us that is envious, ill-willed,
   and inclined to rivalry;
for the avaricious and the grasping, who cannot rest
   until they have their hands on everything,
   and for all within us that is greedy
   and prevents us from sharing and letting others share.

You, Lord, have set out, and you travel through the ages
to reach us in our time.
Come to us also and transform
our pride into humility,
our indolence into courage,
our smugness into disquiet,
our anger into the capacity to make peace,
our lack of love into solicitude,
our envy into sympathy,
our avarice into fullness of life,
and our death into life.
Amen.

KLAUS NAGORNI

**Have mercy on me**

My Lord and my God,
with Bartimaeus I cry out to you: Have mercy on me!
Have mercy on my darkness, and be my Light.
Have mercy on my weakness, and be my Strength.
Have mercy on my loneliness, and be my Friend.
Have mercy on my longing, and be Truth to me.
Call me to you – and I will come!
Amen.

DÖRTE SCHRÖMGES

> Christ asks for a home in your soul, where he can be at rest with you, where he can talk easily to you, where you and he, alone together, can laugh and be silent and be delighted with one another.
>
> CARYL HOUSELANDER

## The other person

Lord, this is the other person,
with whom I do not see eye to eye.
He belongs to you.
You have created him;
you have allowed him, if not wanted him,
to be just as he is.
If you can bear with him, my God,
then I too will bear with him and put up with him,
just as you bear with and put up with me.
Amen.

KARL RAHNER

In forgiving the unforgivable, man comes closest to divine love.

SAINT GERTRUDE THE GREAT

## Each time anew

Each time anew,
O Lord,
you meet the one
who hurts you,
with joy and love.

But I do not respect and honor,
each time anew,
the one who hurts me.

Come to my aid,
each time anew,
so that with you
I may become
one who loves.
Amen.

Based on a prayer by SAINT JOHN OF THE CROSS

# Discerning and deciding

## Father, grant us wisdom

Gracious and holy Father, give us wisdom to perceive you, intelligence to understand you, diligence to seek you, patience to wait for you, eyes to behold you, a heart to meditate on you, and a life to proclaim you; through the power of the Spirit of Jesus Christ our Lord, Amen.

SAINT BENEDICT OF NURSIA

## Seeing things as they really are

O my God,
I want to be able to understand you well.
I beseech you, answer me
when I humbly ask you:
What is truth?
Grant that I may see things as they are,
that I may not allow myself
to be blinded by anything. Amen.

SAINT THÉRÈSE OF LISIEUX

> ” I can nourish myself only on the truth. For this reason I have never longed for visions. On earth we cannot see heaven, the angels as they truly are. I prefer to wait until after my death.
>
> SAINT THÉRÈSE OF LISIEUX

## Solomon's prayer for wisdom

O God of my fathers and Lord of mercy,
who have made all things by your word...
With you is wisdom, who knows your works
and was present when you made the world,
and who understands what is pleasing in your sight
and what is right according to your commandments.
Send her forth from the holy heavens,
and from the throne of your glory send her,
that she may be with me and toil,
and that I may learn what is pleasing to you.

For she knows and understands all things,
and she will guide me wisely in my actions
and guard me with her glory.
[Amen.]

WISDOM 9:1.9–11

[At that time King Solomon said to the LORD:] "I am but a little child; I do not know how to go out or come in.... Give your servant therefore an understanding mind to govern your people, that I may discern between good and evil; for who is able to govern this great people of yours?" It pleased the LORD that Solomon had asked this. And God said to him, "Because you have asked this, and have not asked for yourself long life or riches or the life of your enemies, but have asked for yourself understanding to discern what is right, behold, I now do according to your word. Behold, I give you a wise and discerning mind, so that none like you has been before you and none like you shall arise after you."

1 KINGS 3:7,9–12

## For those seeking understanding

O Creator of the universe,
source of light and wisdom,
thou mighty beginning of all things,
enlighten the dullness of my perception
with the light of thy clarity
and take from me the darkness
of sin and ignorance.

Give me intelligence to understand,
good memory to retain,
the capacity to discern
rightly and thoroughly,
delicacy and exactitude in explanation,
fullness and grace of expression.

Teach the beginning, guide the unfolding, help in the completion,
through Christ, our Lord.
Amen.

Based on a prayer by SAINT THOMAS AQUINAS

## For light to discern by

My God,
what I want to do, I do not do,
and what I do, I do not want to do.
I put things off and cannot decide.
And then, so often, it's too late and already decided,
without my actually deciding anything.
I do not lead my life but am led, as on a leash –
And I don't even know by whom or where to.

Give me, I beg you, your Holy Spirit, your light to discern:
the more important from the less important,
good from evil,
truth from lies,
right from wrong,
the thing perceived from the perception of it,
you, my God, from what I try to make into my god,
your voice from the Babel of human voices,
your glory from the pomp of Satan,
what serves your Kingdom from what is an obstacle to it,
what unites me to you from what separates me from you,
what I possess from what possesses me,
your judgment from my condemnation,
your mercy from my dismissiveness,
fortitude from hard-heartedness,
the eternal from the ephemeral,
the last from the next-to-last,
and the heaven you have given from the one I've made myself.

I reject the voices that would have me believe
that the one cannot be distinguished from the other.

Grant me the goodwill and the capacity,
the courage, and the strength, and the trust,
to decide rightly and to choose
what you have called me to, what you choose to give me,
and what leads me and mine more closely to you. Amen.

GEORG LENGERKE

Beloved, do not believe every spirit, but test the spirits to see whether they are of God; for many false prophets have gone out into the world.

1 JOHN 4:1

**A prayer under pressure**

Dear Lord,
Today is a day like so many others –
with one deadline after another.
Everyone wants something from me,
and there is no time left for me, even to draw breath.

But now is the time, it has to be now – time for you!

How good it is that you know me and love me,
even when I find it hard to love myself.
How good that you do not forget me,
even when I almost forget you, in the troubles of my life.
How good that you always walk beside me,
even when I leave you standing there, somewhere along the way.
How good that you show me a way to walk,
even when I find it so hard to decide myself.
How good that you wish to be my goal,
even when I completely lose my bearings.

The madhouse can wait at the door for a moment,
for a moment the world can hold its breath...
I turn back to you and say:
Thanks be to God!

DÖRTE SCHRÖMGES

# Being called and responding

## The task entrusted to me

God our Father,
how wonderful is your creation. All that is created comes from your hand. I too have been called into being by you, given a task for my life, a task that no one else can fulfill.
I have a mission for life. Maybe I do not recognize this mission clearly on earth, but one day it will become clear to me. I have not come into being without worth or purpose, but as a link in a long chain, a bridge between individuals and generations.
Lord, God, this is the good thing entrusted to me:
To complete your work, to bring peace, to do good, to serve the truth, to live your word, wherever I am, wherever I might be.
Amen.

From the Fiji Islands

> Live what you have understood from the Gospels, even if it is only very little, but realize it fully.
>
> Rule of Taizé

## Grace to choose what leads to my goal

Almighty, eternal God,
you have created me,
together with my brothers and sisters,
for yourself:
to know you,
to love you,
to serve you,
and one day to be with you forever.

All other things on earth
you have given to us, your people,
so that, with their help,
we can live according to your call
and our vocation.

Grant me the vision to recognize
what leads me to you,
so that I may choose it,
and what separates me from you,
so that I may reject it.
Give me your Holy Spirit,
so that I may aspire to and choose
only what leads me more directly to the goal
for which I have been created.
Amen.

Loosely based on *"Principle and Foundation"* in the Spiritual Exercises of SAINT IGNATIUS OF LOYOLA

> Man is created to praise, reverence, and serve God our Lord, and by this means to save his soul. All other things on the face of the earth are created for man to help him fulfill the end for which he is created. From this it follows that man is to use these things to the extent that they will help him to attain his end. Likewise, he must rid himself of them insofar as they prevent him from attaining it.... In all things we should desire and choose only those things which will best help us to attain the end for which we are created.
>
> SAINT IGNATIUS OF LOYOLA, Spiritual Exercises *("Principle and Foundation")*

**Prayer of Saint Francis for discernment**

Most high and glorious God,
enlighten the darkness of my heart
and grant me right faith,
sure hope,
and perfect charity.

Fill me, Lord,
with understanding and knowledge,
that I may fulfill
your holy command.
Amen.

Prayer by SAINT FRANCIS OF ASSISI, before the crucifix in San Damiano

**For vocations**

Holy Father, you call us to be holy,
as you are holy.
We pray to you that in your Church
there may never be lacking holy servants and apostles
who through the Word and the Sacraments
open the path of encounter with you.
Merciful Father,
grant to straying mankind
men and women who,
through the witness of a transfigured life
in the image of your Son,
may joyfully travel,
together with the rest of their brothers and sisters,
toward the heavenly fatherland.
Our Father, with the voice of your Holy Spirit
and trusting in the maternal intercession of Mary,
we call fervently to you:
send your Church priests
who are courageous witnesses of your infinite goodness.
Amen.

BLESSED JOHN PAUL II

## What lies before me today

Good God,
I awake from sleep
and begin a new day with you.
I ask you, open my heart,
to recognize what lies before me today,
to embrace what you give me today
and, with your help, to joyfully do
whatever you ask of me this day.
Amen.

GEORG LENGERKE

## That I may fulfill your loving will

Lord Jesus,
one thing I have asked of you
and will always ask of you,
that I may fulfill your loving will
all the days of my poor
and inadequate life.
Into your hands,
good Lord,
I commend my spirit,
my heart, my memory,
my understanding and my will.
Grant only
that I may serve you with all these,
may love you, be pleasing to you,
and may always praise you.
Amen.

SAINT FRANCIS DE SALES

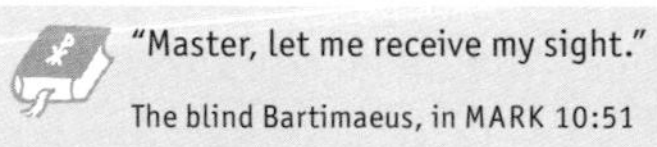

"Master, let me receive my sight."

The blind Bartimaeus, in MARK 10:51

## Let me desire, recognize, and fulfill what pleases you

Almighty God, grant me the grace
to fervently long for what pleases you,
to explore it with wisdom,
to recognize it in truth,
and perfectly fulfill it.

Grant that I may never seek to please,
or fear to displease, anyone but you alone.
Amen.

SAINT THOMAS AQUINAS

## Finding the way to you

Jesus, Son of David, have mercy on me.
Enlighten my eyes,
so that I may find the way to you.
Make my footsteps firm,
so that I do not stray from the path.
Open my mouth,
so that I may speak of you.
You wish me to serve my fellow men.
Let me so serve them
that they find their salvation
and attain to your glory.
Amen.

SAINT ALCUIN OF YORK

> God has assigned to each his place and his responsibilities, and he observes how each one approaches the task he has given him. And he watches over you. Remember this, and perform each deed as though it were directly commanded by God, no matter what it is.
>
> SAINT THEOPHAN THE RECLUSE

## You are calling me

I believe you are calling me to happiness, Lord,
to the new life, to the heaven that begins on earth,
to a state of life, to a mission in the world,
to people and to a community that
reaches up to heaven.

I believe, Lord, that you are calling me,
yet often I do not hear your call.
Let me hear you and understand you in your Word.
Entice me, so that may I seek and find you.
Awaken my longing, so that I may receive you
wherever two or three are gathered in your name.
Send me people who tell me the truth about you,
so that I may hear from you the truth about myself,
about happiness, new life and the heaven
that begins on earth.
Amen.

GEORG LENGERKE

> We must be something great then, since the loving God, who has created and redeemed us, places such value on us.
>
> SAINT JEAN-MARIE VIANNEY, THE CURÉ OF ARS

## The small steps of hope

Jesus, I will not wait; I live the present moment by filling it up with love. A straight line is made up of millions of tiny points that are joined together. My life too is made up of millions of seconds and minutes that are joined together. If I take care to ensure that each point is connected with complete accuracy to the next, then the line will be straight. If I live each minute in perfection, my life will be holy. The path of hope is made up of small steps of hope. The life of hope is made up of the short minutes of hope. Just as you, Jesus, always did what pleased your Father. Every minute I want to speak to you, Jesus; I love you, my life is always a new and eternal bond with you. Every minute I wish to sing with the whole Church: Glory be to the Father and to the Son and to the Holy Spirit.
Amen.

CARDINAL FRANÇOIS-XAVIER (NGUYEN VAN THUAN)

## Send me, Lord

Whom shall I send?
Here I am, Lord.
Send me!

BASED ON ISAIAH 6,8

Send me, Lord,
wherever you please,
for when I am sent by you,
then I am quite sure
that you will help me
– in whatever situation I find myself –
to fulfill what you ask.
Amen.

SAINT FRANCIS DE SALES

# Praying for others – going out to others

## Bearers of peace

Lord, God of peace,
we thank you
for all the longing, all the efforts, all the striving
that your Spirit of peace
kindles in our time.
Open our spirits and our hearts still more
to all our brothers and sisters
who are now in need of love,
so that, more and more,
we may become bearers of peace. Amen.

POPE PAUL VI

> It is not enough, however, to learn prayers by heart. We must live them. Again and again, and tirelessly, we must apply a phrase during the course of the day.
>
> ANTHONY BLOOM

## For my friends

Dear God,
I bring before you my dear ones, my friends
and the particular person whom I love above all others.

Protect them from all evil
and guide them safely on their journey.

Help us to discern
what unites us and what divides us,
what sustains us and what oppresses us,
and who we can, or cannot, be for one another.

Enlighten our sight,
strengthen our hearts,
bless our friendship,
guide our steps
and let us remain in your love.
Amen.

GEORG LENGERKE

## For my parents

God, my Creator,
just as you once placed me
into my parents' arms,
so today I place my parents and their ways
into your arms.
I thank you for their lives.
They bore the pain of birth, of caring and of letting go.
They welcomed me in
and yielded me up.
I ask your love for them.
Amen.

BERNHARD MEUSER

## For the one you choose to give me

Faithful God,
if you will it, I shall one day marry.
Whoever it may be
and wherever he [she] may be,
I pray to you today for this person.
Bless him [her] today and every day,
and protect him [her] from all evil,
let him [her] grow in faith in you,
keep him [her] from false love
and from all harm to body, soul and heart.
Let us both keep watch for each other,
alert, relaxed, and trusting,
and bring us together, as you will.
Amen.

GEORG LENGERKE

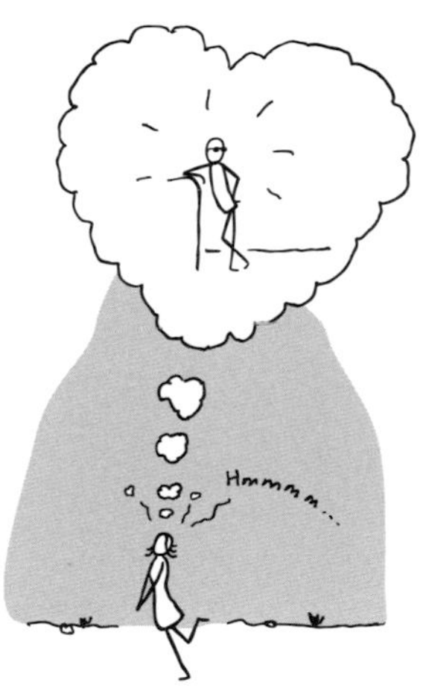


> When two people are silent together, it is always possible that at least one of them is actually praying.
>
> ADRIENNE VON SPEYR

**For someone I have lost**

Dear Lord of the living and the dead,
I bring before you *[name]*,
my dear departed friend,
who was so precious and so close to me,
and whom I miss and mourn.
Thank you for the friendship we shared,
for all we meant to each other,
for all we shared and experienced together,
the joys and sorrows that brought us closer.
Thank you for all that was uniquely him,
for the way he saw the world – and me,
and for the things about him that others could not see.
I pray to you for him:
forgive him in his frailty,
bind up his wounds and comfort him in anguish.
Let nothing in his life have been in vain.
Give him the joy of seeing you and loving you
in the new life that death cannot kill.
And help me now to give him back to you.
For your love is stronger, as you say, than death.
Comfort and console me, and sustain my faith
in the Resurrection of your Son,
until we meet again
in your eternal Light. Amen.

GEORG LENGERKE

**May the angels lead you**

May the angels lead you into paradise.
May the martyrs receive you at your coming
and lead you into the holy city, Jerusalem.
May the choir of angels receive you,
and with Lazarus, who once was poor,
may you have everlasting rest.

*In Paradisum,* from the burial service of the Church

### Loving the unwanted

Dear Lord, you have given me the courage
to trust that you accept me.
Give me also the strength
to love all the unwanted,
just as much as you love me and accept me.

You know, Lord, that the unwanted
are the poorest of the poor.
The rich can also be unwanted,
just as much as the poor of this small earth
that you have given us.

Let us all be sharers
in the riches of your love.
Then we too will be able to accept one another,
in your Kingdom on earth. Amen.

BLESSED TERESA OF CALCUTTA

> Serving means supporting others with our physical bodies, while spiritually knocking on the doors of heaven with our prayers.
>
> SAINT JOHN KLIMAKOS (CLIMACUS)

### To the least of our brethren

> Truly, I say to you, as you did it to one of the least
> of these my brethren, you did it to me.
>
> MATTHEW 25:40

You have gone before me, Lord,
to the least of our brothers and sisters,
to the hungry and the thirsty,
to the stranger and the naked,
to the sick and those in prison.

Take me with you to them, Lord,
so that I can find them and find you with them,
so that they and I can be sisters and brothers again,
and together be with you.

Whatever I do for them
is done with you and also for you.
What we receive from one another
is what you yourself wish to give us.
Wherever we serve one another,
we serve you and your Kingdom,
which none can establish in our midst
but you, and you alone.
Amen.

GEORG LENGERKE

## Open my eyes, Lord

Open my eyes, O Lord,
to the wonders of your love.
With the blind man, I cry out:
Savior, let me see!

Open my ears, O Lord,
to my brothers' cry for help.
Do not let my heart
close up against their need.

Open my hands, O Lord,
for the beggars at my door.
They await their portion too,
Lord grant me the grace to share. Amen.

From the Liturgy of the Hours, German edition

## Against a sharp tongue

Better a blade than a word,
For a blade may at least be blunt.
A knife may sometimes
miss the heart;
A sharp word never does.

HILDE DOMIN

Set a guard over my mouth, O LORD, keep watch over the door of my lips!
Incline not my heart to any evil, to busy myself with wicked deeds
in company with men who work iniquity.

PSALM 141: 3–4

> Your guardian angel came to you from the realm of eternity, when you were reborn as a child of God. Now he goes through life with you and will one day accompany you before the judgment of God. Do not think of him as a weakly being, as so many pictures portray him. He is a mighty spirit, pure as the burning sun, his understanding incorruptibly clear, his will invincible. He is your invisible companion, your living conscience.
>
> ROMANO GUARDINI

## Mighty promise of God

Behold, I send an angel before you,
to guard you on the way
and to bring you to the place
which I have prepared.

EXODUS 23:20

O my guardian angel,
you mighty promise of God.
I have never seen you,
but God tells me you are there.
I have never met you,
(or maybe I've merely forgotten you?)
Yet you have always been there.

Stay with me,
my holy friend,
by day and throughout the night,
whether I am alone or with others.
Stay by my side,
where no one else can walk with me,
where no one else can help me,
where no one else can tell me what to do.

Protect me,
strong helper.
Fight for me.
Shield me from all that can harm me,
and save me from falling.
Amen.

GEORG LENGERKE

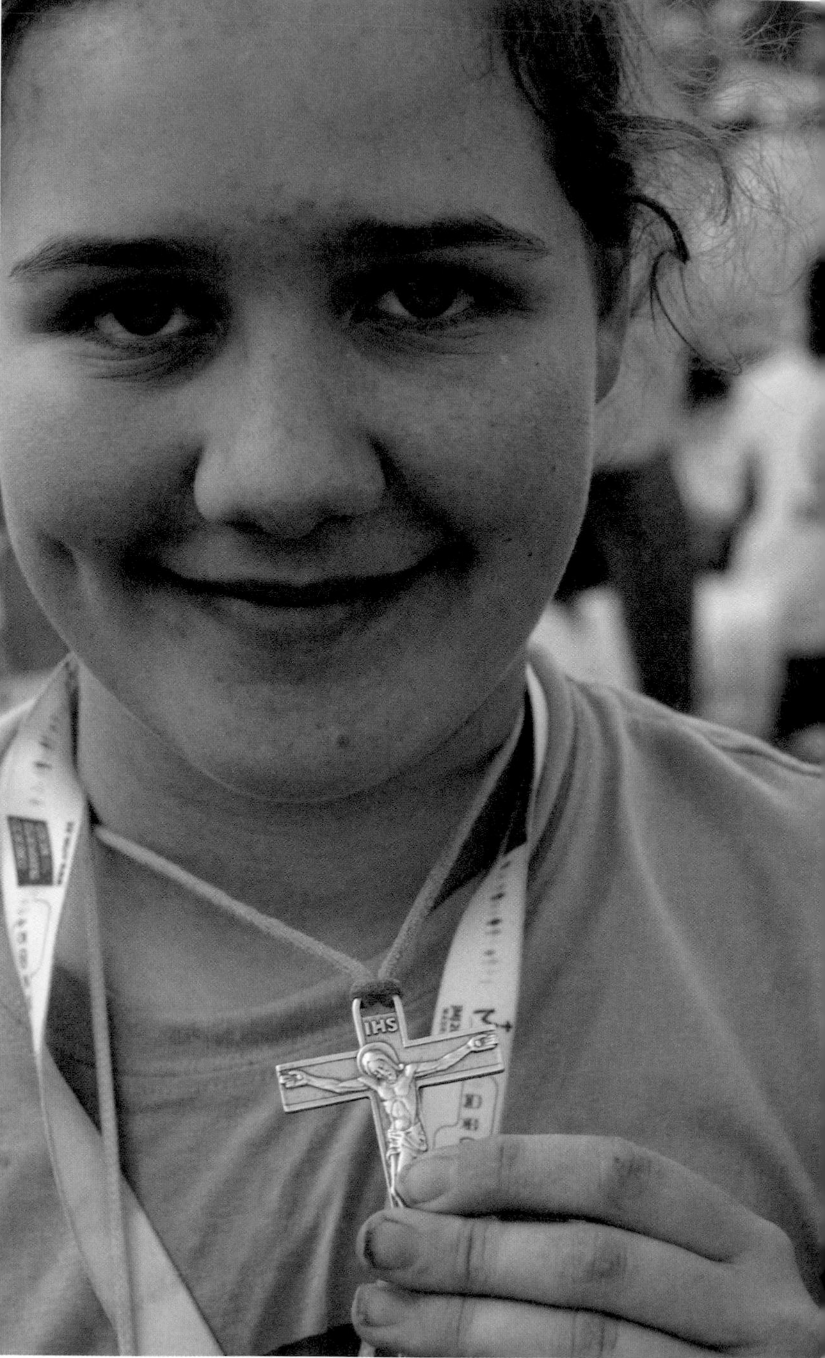

**To my patron saint** (I bear your name)

Dear Saint *[name]*,
Ever since my baptism, I bear your name.
Pray for me to God –
for the strength of your faith,
the breadth of your hope,
the courage of your love.
Support me so that I, like you,
may hear God's loving call today,
and in my life may answer
as God's grace moves me to.
Then one day, with you and all the saints,
may I receive the crown of life.
Amen.

Strictly speaking, we do not worship or adore the saints. Adoration belongs to God alone. But God's Yes to us is an eternal one. He does not will that the dead should remain dead, but that they should live with him. Although separated from them in this world, we remain forever united with them beyond death. Thus our prayers, offered with one another and for one another, likewise reach beyond the Church on earth and beyond death. In praying for the dead, our prayers reach down into death; in our prayers to the saints and blesseds, and in their intercession for us with God, our prayers for one another reach up into heaven.

**Saint Joseph, loving father**

Saint Joseph,
obtain for us the spirit of wisdom,
that it may guide us in all our ways,
in our interior and exterior life.
Care for us, like a loving father,
in all our concerns,
both temporal and eternal,
and especially on this present day,
and for a good death when we die.
Amen.

# Body and life – entrusted to us

## You have given us our bodies

Gracious and merciful God,
You have given us mouths, to speak your praise.
You have given us feet, to walk the path of your salvation.
You have given us knees, to bend reverently before you in prayer.
You have given us hands, to raise in prayer before you,
in thanksgiving and petition,
and through them to bring blessings to our neighbors.
You have given us ears, to listen for your voice.
You have given us a heart, that it may burn for you in love
and direct all our limbs in your service.
Help us to serve you and those around us,
joyfully, and with all our gifts. Amen.

> ❞ Indeed, one who deals ill with himself, what good can he be to anyone? Think about this then: be kind to yourself. I do not say you should do so always, I do not say you should do so often, but I do say you should do so occasionally, from time to time. Be there for yourself also, just as you are for everybody else, or at least be so after everybody else.
>
> SAINT BERNARD OF CLAIRVAUX to Pope Eugene III (letter, *On Consideration*)

## Adorn my heart

Adorn my heart, Lord, with your presence.
Transform it into a dwelling for you!
You are the guest I have been expecting,
the friend who is to stay with me.
For you, for whom a palace would be fitting,
I have only a miserable hut to offer.
I adorn my house with yearning and longing.
Then the shining glory of heaven will light up my dwelling.
My house will be a cathedral, my heart a tabernacle.
Adorn my heart, Lord, with your presence.
Transform it into a dwelling for you. Amen.

BLESSED JOHN XXIII

### Who am I? (Prayer from a prison cell)

Who am I? They often tell me that I emerge from my cell
relaxed and cheerful,
like a lord coming from his castle.

Who am I? They often tell me that I speak with my jailers freely and affably and clearly, as though I were in command.

Who am I? They also tell me that I bear the days of misfortune
with equanimity,
smiling and proud, like someone used to winning.

Am I really what others say I am? Or am I merely what I know myself to be? Restless, nostalgic, sick, like a bird in a cage, struggling to breathe, as though someone were squeezing my throat, hungering for colors, for flowers, for birdsong; thirsting for kind words, for human closeness, quaking with anger at the arbitrary injustice and the pettiest offences, left fretting by the waiting for big things, impotently fearing for friends impossibly far away, too tired and empty to pray, to think, to work; listless and ready to say goodbye to everything?

Who am I? The one or the other?
Am I this one today and tomorrow another?
Am I both at the same time?
A hypocrite to other people, and to myself
a contemptible, snivelling weakling?
Or is what is left in me like a beaten army,
that falls back in disorder from a victory already won?

Who am I? Lonely question that still mocks me.
Whoever I may be, you know me:
I am yours, O God!
Amen.

DIETRICH BONHOEFFER

> When you pray, don't come before God as the person you would like to be. Come before him as the person you really are, as you have actually lived this latest day. Be calm and genuine. And then ask him to bring out the real person in you. For it is already hidden within. He sees it, he knows it, he loves it. He longs for you and is kind to you – unconditionally so.

**Canticle of the Sun**

Most high, all powerful, all good Lord!
All praise is yours, all glory, all honor,
and all blessing.
To you, alone, Most High, do they belong.
No mortal lips are worthy to pronounce your name.

Be praised, my Lord,
through all your creatures,
especially through my lord Brother Sun,
who brings the day; and you give light through him.
And he is beautiful and radiant in all his splendor!
Of you, Most High, he bears the likeness.

Be praised, my Lord,
through Sister Moon and the stars;
in the heavens you have made them
bright, precious and beautiful.

Be praised, my Lord,
through Brothers Wind and Air,
and clouds and storms, and all the weather,
through which you give your creatures sustenance.

Be praised, My Lord,
through Sister Water;
she is very useful, and humble, and precious, and pure.

Be praised, my Lord,
through Brother Fire,
through whom you brighten the night.
He is beautiful and cheerful, and powerful and strong.

Be praised, my Lord,
through our sister Mother Earth,
who feeds us and rules us,
and produces various fruits
with colored flowers and herbs.

Be praised, my Lord,
through those who forgive for love of you;
through those who endure sickness and trial.
Happy those who endure in peace,
for by you, Most High, they will be crowned.

Be praised, my Lord,
through our Sister Bodily Death,
from whose embrace no living person can escape.
Woe to those who die in mortal sin!
Happy those she finds doing your most holy will.
The second death can do no harm to them.

Praise and bless my Lord, and give thanks,
and serve him with great humility.
Amen.

SAINT FRANCIS OF ASSISI

> Adoration should be at the beginning of all our actions and make up a considerable portion of our lives.
>
> BLESSED CHARLES DE FOUCAULD

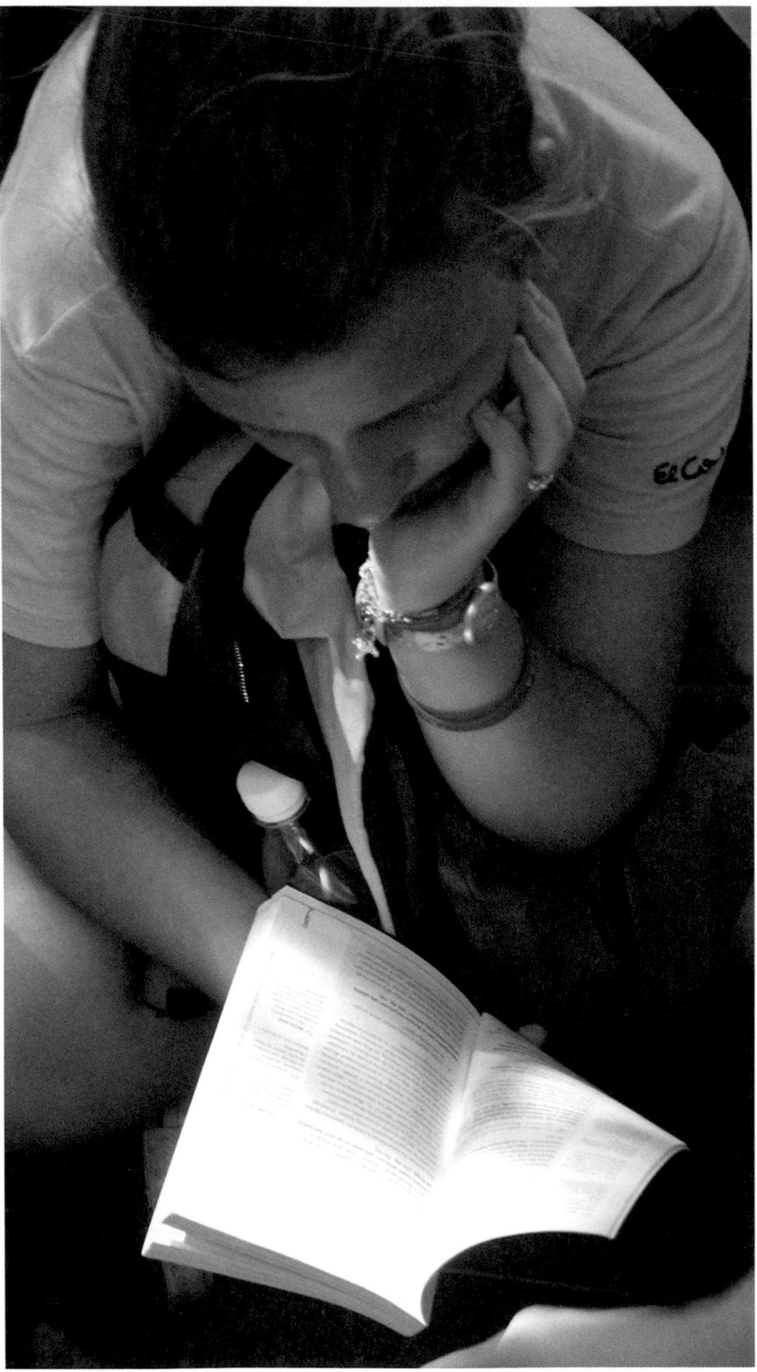

## For strength

There can be no holiness, then, Lord, if you withdraw your supporting hand. No wisdom can be of any help, once you cease to guide it; no courage can support us, if you cease to keep in being. No chastity is secure when you are not its guardian. No, when you leave us, we sink and perish; when you visit us, we are raised up and restored to life. We have no sure footing, but through you we are made firm.

THOMAS À KEMPIS, *Imitation of Christ* (bk. 3, chap. 14)

I ask you then, Lord, stretch out your hand over us.
May you guide us and be our protection. Come to us and raise us up again.
Stay with us and be our constant help, so that we can grow strong and live in you.
Amen.

DÖRTE SCHRÖMGES

## For wisdom

God, give me the courage to change the things I can,
give me the serenity to accept the things I cannot change,
and the wisdom to know the difference.
Amen.

Authorship uncertain, usually attributed to REINHOLD NIEBUHR

## Into your hands

In Him the beginning,
the moon and sun spinning
across the blue fabric of
Heaven's fair tent.

O Father so wise, advise!
Guide and command,
for into your hand
the beginning and end
and all else we present!
Amen.

EDUARD MÖRIKE

**Trusting in your Providence**

O Lord, you have told us
that our Father in heaven will care for us,
just as he cares for the lilies of the field
and the birds of heaven.
You, who did not even have a place
to lay your weary head,
be our teacher.

Teach us to trust in God's providence,
and help us to overcome our human greed.
For greed never made anyone happy.

Give us the strength to give ourselves totally to you,
and so be an instrument
to fulfill your will.

Bless the use of money in the world,
so that the hungry may be fed,
the naked clothed, the poor sheltered,
and the sick cared for.

And grant us, Lord, your Holy Spirit,
so that we may clearly recognize,
through the faith you grant us,
that we are all worth more in your sight
than any beautiful lily
or any singing skylark in the air.
Amen.

BLESSED TERESA OF CALCUTTA

## Entangled in the Web

Lord, Creator of the real world,
I bring before you all I find on the Internet:
the many words – both true and false,
the many people – near and far,
the many details – important and trivial,
The many images – of the best and the worst in man.

Free me – where I've become entangled in the Web.
Heal me – where its images have wounded my soul.
Lead me back to the truth – where I've been led astray.

Help me to distinguish
the virtual from the real world,
to choose wisely the things that really matter,
to resist firmly all manipulation,
to use with measure what is set before me,
and bravely live my daily life with you.

GEORG LENGERKE

## Calling in time of need

### Heavy-hearted

Living God, you know how heavy my heart is,
and how tight my chest.
I can't find a way out.
Help me, my God!
I know you care for me and love me,
and that you allow each trial I face.
I know you turn all things to good for me.
But help me –
do not let this fear overwhelm me.
I entrust this day to you,
and all my life.
Guide me where you will
and how you know is best for me.
For whether I live or die,
I am with you, and you are with me, my God. Amen.

DÖRTE SCHRÖMGES

> ! We are not responsible for the wounds that others inflict on us. But we are responsible for dealing with them in the right way. We must first wish, then pray, and finally allow the Father, through our wounded Savior, to make our wounds his own, and so heal them.

### Strengthen hope in us

We beg you, God of grace and eternal life,
increase and strengthen hope in us.
Grant us this virtue of the strong,
this strength of the confident,
this courage of the unshakeable.
Then we can boldly grasp, again and again,
the challenges in our lives.
Then we will be filled with cheerful confidence
that we do not work in vain.
Then we can do our work and know that you
– without us and where our strength may fail –
still work your glory and our salvation,
according to your good purpose.
Strengthen in us your hope.
Amen.

KARL RAHNER

### Come to us

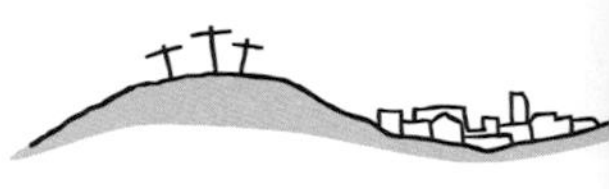

Come to us, O God, when the night surrounds us!
Come to us in the night of disappointment,
Come to us in the night of guilt,
Come to us in the night of fear,
Come to us in the night of hatred,
Come to us in the night of loneliness,
Come to us in the night of lost love,
Come to us in the night of anxiety,
Come to us in the night of pain,
Come to us in the night of questioning,
Come to us in the night of rejection,
Come to us in the night of broken relationships,
Come to us in the night of despair,
Come to us in the night of hopelessness,
Come to us in the night of death.

Come to me in my night
and stay with me, my God,
in every night. Amen.

### In sickness

Lord, I have time. A great deal of time.
When I was healthy, I thought how beautiful it would be
to have plenty of time.

Now I do have time, necessarily so.
But these hours and days
are another kind of time.
Time to think and time to ponder,
to question, and to make reproaches too.
So many things are going through my head.

Lord, I need you.
Help me to keep courageous, trusting, and confident
in your goodness to us, your children.
May you be our God, in joy and suffering. Amen.

BLAISE PASCAL

Fear knocked at the door. Faith answered. And lo, no one was there.

Author unknown

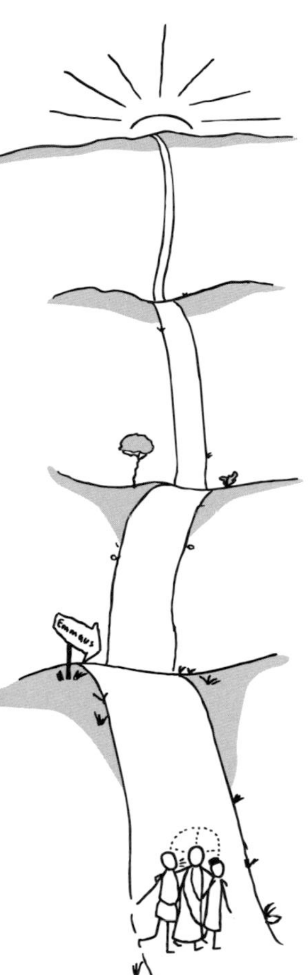


## On the road to Emmaus

My eyes are locked in,
my memory trapped and in chains.
Imprisoned in the horror experienced,
like the loop of a recurring film.

My hopes are utterly dashed,
my faith is disillusioned,
my love has been fooled and shamed,
crucified and derided,
and even its body has been stolen.

Behind me, my Jerusalem.
I look back to the town
in frozen horror.
Before me, an Emmaus,
with some lodgings, somewhere
on the way to nowhere.

Tell me, unknown traveler,
what really happened there?
And who was it that I believed in?

Help me, mysterious teacher,
unlock my frozen gaze,
and open up the door
of my imprisoned memory.

Stay with me, strange friend,
for evening is near
and my day is almost done –

unless you break the Bread for me,
and open my eyes to recognize You. Amen.

GEORG LENGERKE (see Luke 24:1–35)

Stay with us, for it is toward evening and the day is now far spent.

The disciples on the road to Emmaus, LUKE 24:29

These words of the Gospel are the first prayer addressed by the Church to the risen Christ. It is a prayer – without even being aware of it – an everyday phrase that springs from a deep emotion, gratitude, joy, and a profound yearning and concern combined. Rarely was a more beautiful prayer uttered.

HEINRICH SPAEMANN

### Wherever I go, you are there

Where shall I go from your Spirit?
Or where shall I flee from your presence?
If I ascend to heaven, you are there!
If I make my bed in Sheol, you are there!
If I take the wings of the morning
and dwell in the uttermost parts of the sea,
even there your hand shall lead me,
and your right hand shall hold me.
If I say, "Let only darkness cover me,
and the light about me be night,"
even the darkness is not dark to you,
the night is bright as the day;
for darkness is as light with you.
[Glory be to the Father, and to the Son,
and to the Holy Spirit, as it was in the beginning,
is now, and ever shall be,
world without end. Amen.]

PSALM 139:7–12

> ! We don't need to run away from God. And indeed we cannot. He comes after us – even into the outermost darkness, even to the Cross, and even into those places where nobody wants to acknowledge God any more and darkness thinks it has triumphed over the Light.

### When men are wolves

When things get really tough for me,
when fear grips at my throat,
when there is no way out that I can see,
when men are wolves,
and I writhe like a miserable worm,
Then, Lord, put the right words into my mouth.
Then, Lord, lead me out of this corner into the open.
Then, Lord, give me hope in the midst of my fear.
Then, Lord, show me the way into freedom.
Amen.

DÖRTE SCHRÖMGES (inspired by Esther 14:1–19.)

### Short prayers from the heart

Father, into your hands I commit my spirit!

LUKE 23:46

Jesus, Son of David, have mercy on me!

MARK 10:47

I rest like a child in your arms, O LORD.

Based on PSALM 131:2

Whether I live or whether I die, I belong to the Lord.

Based on ROMANS 14:8

Lord, to whom shall we go? You have the words of eternal life.

JOHN 6:68

My Lord and my God!

JOHN 20:28

[Lord,] stay with us, for it is toward evening and the day is now far spent.

LUKE 24:29

Come, Lord Jesus!

REVELATION 22:20

My Lord and my God, strengthen me in this hour!

Have mercy on me, Lord, for I am weak!

You in me, and I in you.

# Being mortal, yet immortal

## You are my beginning and my end

> I am the Alpha and the Omega,
> the first and the last,
> the beginning and the end.
>
> REVELATION 22:13

You are my Alpha and my Omega,
my first and my last,
my beginning and my end.
Before my beginning, you were;
After my ending, you will be;
and until then
– yesterday, today, tomorrow –
You are; present here,
wanting to come to me,
giving me life,
giving yourself.
*Maranatha* – Come, Lord Jesus!

GEORG LENGERKE

> ” The Aramaic prayer *Maranatha* can be read – and hence understood – in two ways: *Marana tha* ("Lord, come!") or *Maran atha* ("the Lord has come"). This duality beautifully reflects the Christian understanding and expectation of Jesus' coming, for it is both the expectant cry "Come, Lord!" and the grateful acclamation "He has come!"
>
> POPE BENEDICT XVI

## Prompt our actions with your grace

Lord, be the beginning and end
of all that we do and say.
Prompt our actions with your grace,
and complete them
with your all-powerful help.
Amen.

From the Liturgy of the Hours

## Our heart is restless

You are great, O Lord, and greatly to be praised:
great is your power
and your wisdom is without measure.
And man, so small a part of your creation,
wants to praise you:
this man, though clothed with mortality
and bearing the evidence of sin
and the proof that you withstand the proud.
Despite everything, man,
though but a small part of your creation,
wants to praise you.
You yourself encourage him to delight in your praise,
for you have made us for yourself,
and our heart is restless until it rests in you.

SAINT AUGUSTINE OF HIPPO, *Confessions*

> ❞ Piety means "seeking God's face"; it means living turned toward his face. It thereby accords with the meaning of creation, just as Saint Augustine has expressed it: "You have made us for yourself".
>
> ROMANO GUARDINI

## After a seemingly wasted day

O my Jesus,
when I think of your words:

> Behold, I am coming soon, bringing my recompense, to repay every one for what he has done
>
> (REVELATION 22:12),

then you will find it very awkward when you come to me.
I have no good works!
So you will not be able to repay me according to my works, and then you will simply have to repay me according to your works.

SAINT THÉRÈSE OF LISIEUX

> ❞ And even if I had nothing to offer him, as on this evening, then I would simply give him this nothing.
>
> SAINT THÉRÈSE OF LISIEUX

## At the going down of the sun

God, who created
the clear light of day,
we celebrate your glory, Lord,
at the going down of the sun.

Now the evening sun swiftly sets,
enfolding the world in darkness
according to his ordained path.

Truly, Almighty Lord, you do not
allow your supplicating servants
to be oppressed by the darkness
of their daily labors.

Let not the light of day
depart from our confused minds,
but let us, shielded by thy grace,
perceive your kindly light.

Be near, merciful Father,
and your co-equal Son
and with the Holy Spirit
reign over us for evermore.
Amen.

Based on *Deus, qui claro lumine* (seventh/eighth century)

Then Job arose, ... and he said, "Naked I came from my mother's womb, and naked shall I return; the LORD gave and the LORD has taken away; blessed be the name of the LORD."

JOB 1:20,21

## At the end of the day

My God, each evening
I come joyfully to you
to thank you for the graces you have given me.
I ask pardon for the faults I have committed
during this day, which now fades like a dream.

Jesus, how happy I would be
if I had always been faithful.
Yet unfortunately I am often sad in the evening,
for I feel I could have responded better to your grace.

But I will not lose courage
at the sight of my misery,
but instead I come trustfully to you.
For I think, it is not the healthy
who need the doctor, but the sick.
And so I implore you
to heal me and forgive me.

And tomorrow, with the help of your grace,
I will begin a new life,
in which every moment
is to be a sign
of love and gratitude.
And one day, after I have knelt
evening after evening before your altar,
there will come
the final evening of my life.
And then for me the everlasting day will dawn,
that knows no evening anymore.
Then, on your divine heart, I will rest
from all the battles of this heart.
Amen.

SAINT THÉRÈSE OF LISIEUX

> ! Praying to reach your goal in life with God and praying to be shown the way there belong together. The journey is not the goal. But, in thinking of the heavenly goal, you should not forget the earthly way there. When you pray, do not attempt to pray your way for Jesus' sake out of your own real life. For Jesus came so that your life could be his life too! So instead pray with him, rooted in your true and real daily life. In this way everyday life with him becomes the way along which his goal comes to meet you.

### Into your hands, dear Lord

Into your hands, dear Lord, I return this day.
You have given it to me, now I give it back to you.
Preserve in me what you have given me.
May the seed sprout that you have sown today,
and may you complete what I was only able to begin.

## Nunc dimittis

Lord, now let your servant depart in peace,
according to your word;
For my eyes have seen your salvation
which you have prepared in the presence of all peoples,
a light for revelation to the Gentiles,
and for glory to your people Israel.
[Glory be to the Father, and to the Son, and to the Holy Spirit,
as it was in the beginning, is now, and ever shall be, world without end.
Amen.]

LUKE 2:29–32, Prayer of the elderly Simeon at the presentation of the Child Jesus in the Temple.

## Remind me, Lord

> Grant us to sit, one at your right hand
> and one at your left, in your glory.
>
> James and John to Jesus, MARK 10:37

Sometimes, Lord, it strikes a chord,
this longing of your disciples for heaven,
and their anxious queries as to whether
it will all turn out right in the end.

Remind me of heaven, Lord,
and as I think about the destination,
don't let me forget the way
by which my destination comes to meet me.

Remind me of your kingdom, Lord,
and as I imagine how it will be,
don't let me forget the here and now
in which your kingdom has to start.

Remind me of your coming, Lord,
and don't let me, in living my life,
forget your dying,
through which you choose to live with me.

Remind me of your promise, Lord,
that everything will turn out right,
because you have made my story
your own as well. Amen.

GEORG LENGERKE

## You yourself will be our Judge

Just look at us, Lord...
Day after day we drag one another
before the tribunal of our own unforgiving
and deliver our relationships the death sentence.
But you yourself will be the Judge
of the living and of the dead.

I renounce and yield to you
the final judgment –
on the people around me,
on my parents and siblings,
on my acquaintances and friends,
on those I love and those I loathe,
on those who owe to me
   and those to whom I owe,
on those I am cut off from
   and those I am caught up with.
I leave them all to your final judgment
and ask that you be merciful to them.

I also renounce and yield to you
the final judgement
on myself,
the daily, unforgiving sentence that I pass within me.
May you be my Judge each day,
for you alone are just and merciful.
Amen.

GEORG LENGERKE

# Praying with the Mother of Jesus

## Mary, you said Yes

Mary, Mother of the Yes,
you listened to Jesus and
know the sound of his voice
and the beating of his heart.
You Morning Star, speak to us about him
and tell us how you follow him
on the way of faith.

Mary, you lived in Nazareth
together with Jesus.
Imprint on our lives your feelings,
your docility, your silence,
that listens and,
in truly free decisions,
brings the Word to blossoming.

Mary, tell us about Jesus,
so that our faith in its freshness
may shine from our eyes
and warm the hearts of those we meet,
just as you did when you went to visit Elizabeth
and she, old as she was,
rejoiced with you over the gift of life.
Mary, Virgin of the Magnificat,
help us to bring joy into the world
and, as you did in Cana,
encourage all young people
engaged in the service of their brethren,
to do only what Jesus tells them.
Mary, turn your gaze upon young people,
so that they may become a fruitful soil
of the Church.

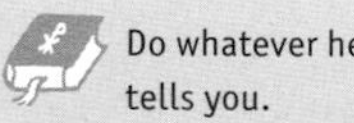

Do whatever he tells you.

Mary, at the marriage in Cana, JOHN 2:5

Behold, I am the handmaid of the Lord; let it be to me according to your word.

Mary, at the Annunciation, LUKE 1:38

Pray that Jesus, who died and rose again,
may be reborn in us and transform us,
in a night full of light, fully filled by him.
Mary, Mother of God and gate of heaven,
help us to lift up our gaze.
We want to see Jesus; to speak with him;
to proclaim his love to all.

POPE BENEDICT XVI

## Who you are

Mary,
Foretaste of heaven
Tender radiance,
Morning hymn,
Fragrance of our homeland,
Warming hand,
Sister,
Friend,
Smile of heaven.

BERNHARD MEUSER

## Mother, you remained faithful

Holy Mary, Mother of the Lord,
You remained faithful when the disciples fled.
Just as you believed, when the angel announced the incredible –
your destiny as Mother of the Most High –
So too you believed, in the hour of his utter humiliation.
So you became – in the hour of the Cross,
in the hour of this world's darkest night –
Mother of believers, Mother of the Church.
We ask you, teach us to believe, and help our faith to become
courage for service and acts of supportive and sympathetic love.
Amen.

POPE BENEDICT XVI

When Jesus saw his mother, and the disciple whom he loved standing near, he said to his mother, "Woman, behold your son!" Then he said to the disciple, "Behold your mother!" And from that hour the disciple took her to his own home.

JOHN 19:26–27

### Look upon us

Dearest Mother, look awhile,
on your trusting people smile,
who honor you, their Mother dear,
and seek your help and comfort here.

Bless us in your heart so pure,
comfort us in all our fear,
stay by us in all our need,
show us Jesus, when we're freed.

SAINT HILDEGARD OF BINGEN

### Salve Regina – Hail, holy Queen

Hail, holy Queen,
Mother of mercy;
Hail, our life, our sweetness
and our hope!
To thee do we cry, poor banished children of Eve;
to thee do we send up our sighs,
mourning and weeping in this vale of tears.
Turn then, O most gracious advocate,
thine eyes of mercy toward us;
and after this our exile, show unto us
the blessed fruit of thy womb, Jesus.
O clement, O loving, O sweet Virgin Mary.

HERMANN VON REICHENAU / SAINT BERNARD OF CLAIRVAUX

### Alma Redemptoris Mater – Loving Mother of the Redeemer

Loving Mother of our Savior,
hear thou thy people's cry,
Star of the deep, and portal of the sky!
Mother of him who thee from nothing made,
sinking we strive, and called to thee for aid.
Oh, by that joy which Gabriel brought to thee,
thou Virgin first and last, let us thy mercy see.

HERMANN VON REICHENAU

### Memorare

Remember, O most gracious Virgin Mary,
That never was it known that anyone who fled to thy protection,
Implored thy help,
Or sought thine intercession was left unaided.

Inspired by this confidence, I fly unto thee, O Virgin of virgins, my mother
To thee do I come, before thee I stand, sinful and sorrowful.
O Mother of the Word Incarnate, despise not my petitions, but in thy mercy hear and answer me.

Already in the Scriptures, Our Lady is portrayed as Queen of Heaven:

And a great sign appeared in heaven, a woman clothed with the sun, with the moon under her feet, and on her head a crown of twelve stars.

REVELATIONS 12:1

### My soul – your dwelling

Living God,
in your grace
you make the soul of the believer
greater than the heavens.
For the heavens and all the other creatures
cannot comprehend you,
the Creator of all things.
But my soul desires to be for you
a dwelling and a resting place.

As the Virgin Mary bore you in her womb,
so I desire to bear you in my heart.
I wish to make a dwelling for you
in the chambers of my heart and soul.
I wish to follow in the footsteps of your Mother, Mary,
in self-giving, humility, and poverty.

Christ, I wish to contain you,
just as you contain me and all the world.
You are my true riches,
and nothing in the world
is as precious as you. Amen.

Based on a prayer by SAINT CLARE OF ASSISI

### Salutation of the Blessed Virgin Mary

Hail, O Lady, holy Queen, Mary, holy Mother of God.
You are the Virgin made church and the one chosen by the most holy Father in heaven, whom he consecrated with his most holy beloved Son and with the Holy Spirit, the Paraclete, in whom there was and is all the fullness of grace and every good.
Hail, his Palace!
Hail, his Tabernacle!
Hail, his Home!
Hail, his Robe!
Hail, his Servant!
Hail, his Mother!

SAINT FRANCIS OF ASSISI

### Regina Coeli – Queen of Heaven, rejoice

O Queen of Heaven rejoice! Alleluia!
For he whom you did merit to bear, alleluia!
Has risen as he said. Alleluia!
Pray for us to God.
Alleluia!

## The Rosary

**Step 1:** Start on the cross/crucifix with:
*+ In the name of the Father, and of the Son, and of the Holy Spirit. Amen.*
*I believe ...* (Apostles' Creed, see p. 88)

**Step 2:** Then, on the first small bead after the cross:
*Our Father, who art in heaven...*

**Step 3:** Then, on each of the next three small beads:
*Hail Mary, full of grace, the Lord is with thee. Blessed art thou among women, and Blessed is the fruit of thy womb, Jesus.*
*Holy Mary, Mother of God, pray for us sinners, now and at the hour of our death. Amen.*
[According to various different traditions, these three Hail Marys can be offered:
a) for the virtues of Faith, Hope, and Love,
b) in honor of the three Persons of the Trinity – Father, Son, and Holy Spirit,
c) in honor of Our Blessed Lady, as Daughter of the eternal Father, Mother of the divine Son and Spouse of the Holy Spirit.]

**Step 4:** Then, the *Glory Be:*
*Glory be to the Father, and to the Son, and to the Holy Spirit,*
*as it was in the beginning, is now, and ever shall be, world without end. Amen.*

**Step 5:** Then, the five decades (one *Our Father,* followed by ten *Hail Marys,* followed by one *Glory be*). It is customary, while reciting them, to meditate on the Mysteries of Our Lord's life, as set out below:

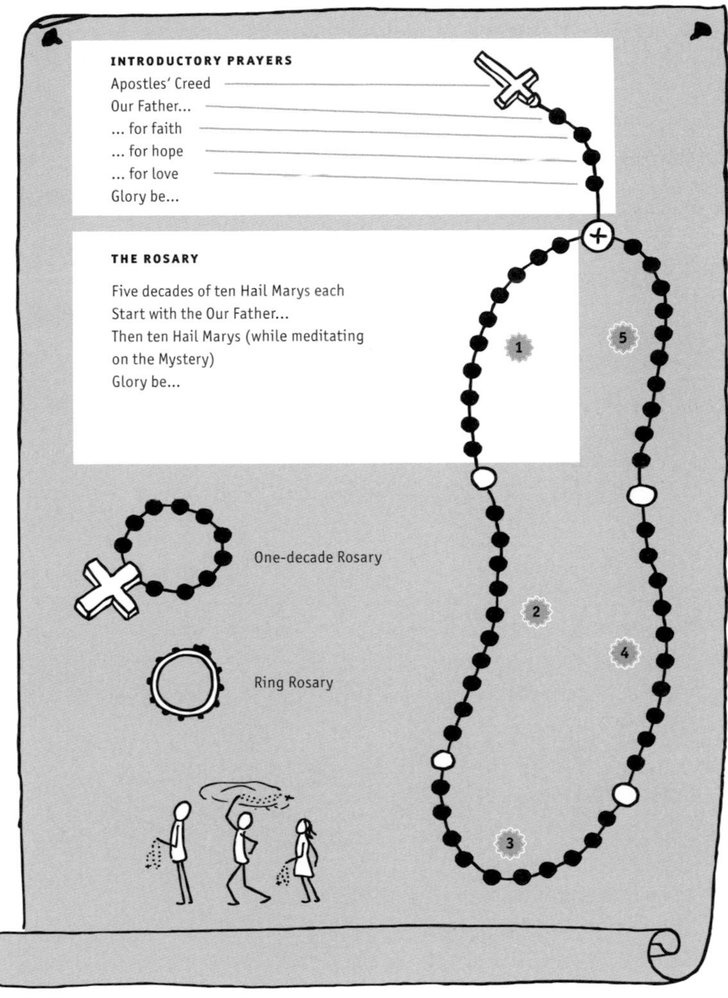


> Ever since my childhood and youth this prayer has held an important place in my spiritual life. The prayer of the Rosary has accompanied me in moments of joy and trial. Many are the cares I have included in this prayer, and through it have always drawn strength and comfort.
>
> BLESSED JOHN PAUL II

> If you do not know how you should pray, then ask him to teach you, and ask his heavenly Mother to pray with you and for you. The Rosary can help you to learn the art of prayer, with the simplicity and profundity of Mary.
>
> POPE BENEDICT XVI

**The Joyful Mysteries (the events surrounding the birth and early life of Jesus)**

1. The Annunciation (LUKE 1:35)
2. The Visitation (LUKE 1:39–56)
3. The Nativity (LUKE 2:1–20)
4. The Presentation of the Child Jesus in the Temple (LUKE 2:22–24)
5. The Finding of Jesus in the Temple (LUKE 2:41–52)

**The Luminous Mysteries (scenes from the public life of Jesus) [optional]**

1. The Baptism of Jesus by John in the River Jordan (LUKE 3:21–22)
2. The Wedding Feast at Cana (JOHN 2:1–12)
3. The Proclamation of the Kingdom, with the Call to Conversion (MATTHEW 9:35)
4. The Transfiguration (LUKE 9:28–36)
5. The Institution of the Holy Eucharist (MARK 14:17–25)

**The Sorrowful Mysteries (the passion and death of Christ)**

1. The Agony in the Garden (LUKE 22:44)
2. The Scourging at the Pillar (JOHN 19:1)
3. The Crowning with Thorns (JOHN 19:2)
4. The Carrying of the Cross (JOHN 19:17)
5. The Crucifixion (JOHN 17:18)

**The Glorious Mysteries (Easter, Pentecost, Our Lady)**

1. The Resurrection (LUKE 24:6)
2. The Ascension (ACTS 1:9–11)
3. The Descent of the Holy Spirit (ACTS 2:1–13)
4. The Assumption of Our Lady (1 CORINTHIANS 15:22–23)
5. The Coronation of Our Lady as Queen of Heaven and Earth (REVELATION 12:1)

> The Rosary ... is at heart a Christocentric prayer. In the sobriety of its elements, it has all the depth of the Gospel message in its entirety, of which it can be said to be a compendium. ... With the Rosary, the Christian people sits at the school of Mary and is led to contemplate the beauty on the face of Christ and to experience the depths of his love. Through the Rosary the faithful receive abundant grace, as though from the very hands of the Mother of the Redeemer.
>
> BLESSED JOHN PAUL II *(Rosarium Virginis Mariae, 1)*

# Glossary of names

**Alcuin of York, Saint** (735–804). Anglo-Saxon, Benedictine abbot, and adviser to Charlemagne; taught many great figures of his age. **126**

**Alphanus of Salerno** (ca. 1015/1020–1085). Benedictine abbot, poet, and physician. **68**

**Ambrose of Milan, Saint** (339–397). Bishop of Milan, theologian, administrator, and Doctor of the Church. 37, **83,** 90–91, **118**

**Augustine of Hippo, Saint** (354–430). Bishop, spiritual writer, theologian, and Doctor of the Church. **22, 32, 36, 50, 101, 107, 153**

**Benedict of Nursia, Saint** (480–547). Hermit, then founder of Benedictine order and author of its Rule; highly influential for later religious orders. 33, **118**

**Benedict XVI, Pope** (Joseph Ratzinger, *1927). Priest, archbishop, and theologian; elected Pope in 2005. 15, 54, 60, 64, 72, 78, 101, 152, **158–159,** 165

**Bernanos, Georges** (1888–1948). French Catholic writer. 44, 106

**Bernard of Clairvaux, Saint** (1090–1153). French Cistercian abbot, preacher, and mystic; greatly influenced political events of his time. **99,** 138, **161**

**Bloom, Anthony** (1914–2003). Russian Orthodox monk, bishop, and spiritual writer. 15, 131

**Bonhoeffer, Dietrich** (1906–1945). German Lutheran pastor and theologian; opposed Hitler, imprisoned, and executed in Flossenbürg concentration camp. **45, 66, 139**

**Buber, Martin** (1878–1965). Jewish philosopher and writer on religion. 26

**Catherine of Siena, Saint** (1347–1380). Italian lay Dominican, mystic, and Doctor of the Church; renowned for her letters to major figures of her time. 109

**Chardin, Pierre Teilhard de** (1881–1955). French Jesuit and palaeontologist. **30**

**Charles de Foucauld, Blessed** (1858–1916). Wild youth, then deep conversion as soldier in Africa; became monk, priest, and hermit among Muslim Tuareg in Sahara; later died there as martyr. **107,** 141

**Claudel, Paul** (1868–1955). French poet and dramatist. **112**

**Clare of Assisi** (1193/1194–1253). Italian; at the age of eighteen followed Saint Francis of Assisi in his radical new monastic way of life; foundress of the Poor Clares. **162**

**Claudius, Matthias** (1740–1815). German poet and journalist. **93**

**Delp, Alfred** (1907–1945). German Jesuit theologian and writer; executed for resistance to Third Reich. 49

**Domin, Hilde** (1909–2006). German poet. **134**

**Eckhart, Meister** (ca. 1260–1326). German Dominican mystic and spiritual writer. 24

**Ephrem the Syrian, Saint** (ca. 306–373). Great poet of early Church whose mystical writings often merge into prayer and praise; Doctor of the Church. 52

**Faustina Kowalska, Saint** (1905-1938). Polish nun and mystic who experienced the revelations of Divine Mercy. **97**

**Francis de Sales, Saint** (1567–1622). French Bishop of Geneva and outstanding pastor of post-Reformation era; religious founder and Doctor of the Church. 14, 97, **125, 129**

**Francis of Assisi, Saint** (1182–1226). Italian; renounced father's wealth at age twenty-four to "follow naked the naked Christ"; founder of Franciscan Order, mystic, and renowned for sense of unity with all God's creatures. **74, 124, 140–141, 163**

**François-Xavier** (Nguyen Van Thuan, 1928–2002). Vietnamese priest, bishop, and cardinal who spent thirteen years in prison for his faith and nine in solitary confinement. **129**

**Gertrude the Great, Saint** (1256–1301/1302). German Benedictine, mystic, and theologian; renowned mystic, Scripture scholar, and spiritual counselor. 13, 58

**Guardini, Romano** (1885–1968). Italian Catholic priest and philosopher; profoundly influenced liturgical and youth movements of his time in Germany. 12, **21,** 66, 71, 107, 135, 153

**Hammarskjöld, Dag** (1905–1961). Swedish politician and writer; United Nations General Secretary and Nobel peace prize winner. **106**

**Hermann von Reichenau** (Hermann the Cripple, 1013-1054). Benedictine monk on island of Reichnau, Lake Constance, Germany. Poet, musician, teacher and polymath. **160**

**Hildegard of Bingen, Saint** (1098–1179). German Benedictine abbess, poet, musician, mystic, natural healer, and sought-after counselor. **103, 161**

**Höfer, Alfons** (b. 1937). German Jesuit priest and theologian. **42**

**Houselander, Caryll** (1901-1954). English laywoman, artist, poet, popular religious writer, and mystic. 116

**Ignatius of Loyola, Saint** (1491–1556). Founder of the Society of Jesus (Jesuits), important teacher of the spiritual life, and author of the *Spiritual Exercises.* **55, 123**

**Irenaeus of Lyons, Saint** (c. 135-c. 202). Important Father of the early Church. 21

**Jean-Marie Vianney, Saint,** (Curé of Ars, 1786-1859). Simple French priest renowned for his holiness and wisdom in the confessional; patron of priests. 28, **109,** 127, 147

**John Henry Newman, Blessed** (1801–1890). English Catholic convert from Anglicanism, cardinal, renowned writer, theologian, and philosopher. 30, **31, 48,** 57, **96**

**John Klimakos (Climacus), Saint** (525–c. 606). Greek monk, hermit, ascetic, and writer. 133

**John Paul II, Blessed** (Karol Wojtyla, 1920–2005). Polish theologian, bishop, and Pope from 1978 to 2005. Charismatic spiritual leader; played crucial role in collapse of communism; founder of World Youth Days. **56,** 63, **77, 124,** 165, 166

**John of the Cross, Saint** (1542–1591). Spanish Carmelite priest, poet, and mystic; Doctor of the Church. **44, 117**

**John XXIII, Blessed.** (Angelo Giuseppe Roncalli, 1881–1963). Patriarch of Venice; Pope from 1958 till 1963; called Second Vatican Council. **138**

**Schutz, Roger** (1915–2005). Founder and prior of the ecumenical community of Taizé in France. **65, 113**

**Spaemann, Heinrich** (1903–2001). German, art historian, former radical atheist, Catholic convert, priest, and writer. 38, 85, 89, 102, 149

**Speyr, Adrienne von** (1902–1967). Swiss doctor, Catholic convert, mystic, and spiritual writer. 131

**Spurgeon, Charles Haddon** (1834–1892). English Baptist, influential preacher, and writer. 12

**Tauler, Johannes** (c. 1300–1361). German Dominican, preacher, and mystic. **67**

**Teresa of Avila, Saint** (1515–1582). Spanish Carmelite, reformer of her order, mystic, and Doctor of the Church. 23, 40, 46, 59, 109

**Teresa Benedicta of the Cross, Saint** (Edith Stein, 1891–1942). German Jewish philosopher; Catholic convert and Carmelite nun; martyred in Auschwitz with her sister Rosa. **75**

**Teresa of Calcutta, Blessed** (Mother Teresa, 1910–1997). Albanian nun; foundress of the Missionaries of Charity; cared for poor and dying in Calcutta, India; awarded Nobel Peace Prize. 34, **96,** 107, **133, 144**

**Theophan the Recluse, Saint** (1815–1894). Russian Orthodox priest, monk, hermit, scholar, and teacher. 37, 126

**Thérèse of Lisieux, Saint** (1873–1897). French Carmelite nun, mystic, and author of the "Little Way" of childlike simplicity; declared a Doctor of the Church for her profound spirituality. **39,** 75, **118,** 118, **153,** 153, **154–155**

**Thomas Aquinas, Saint** (1225–1277). Italian Dominican priest and scholar, towering figure of the Middle Ages, Doctor of the Church, and one of the greatest theologians. **47, 72, 108, 119, 126**

**Thomas à Kempis** (1379/1380–1471). German Augustinian monk, priest and mystical writer. Author of the *Imitation of Christ*. **143**

# Index of prayers

YOUCAT.org

http://youcat.org/

About the Church

I believe

YOUCAT Video

YOUCAT Study Groups

Study this Catechism!
This is my heartfelt desire...
Form study groups and networks;
share with each other on the Internet!

POPE BENEDICT XVI
Foreword to the YOUCAT

# www.youcat.org

**KNOW. SHARE. MEET. EXPRESS.**

- Information and ideas on the YOUCAT
- Regularly updated witness by young people
- Study groups for learning about all aspects of the Catholic faith
- Creative portal for film, music, artwork, etc
- And much more besides...

## Acknowledgments

Sources used for the German edition (and used in translation in the English edition):
Page 106: Dag Hammarskjöld, *Zeichen am Weg* © 2011, Verlag Freies Geistesleben and Urachhaus GmbH, Stuttgart.
Pages 45, 66, 139: Dietrich Bonhoeffer, *Widerstand und Ergebung* © 1998, Gütersloher Verlagshaus, Gütersloh, part of the Random House publishing group GmbH.
Page 104: *Es ist Zeit zur Aussaat,* a novena for vocations to the priestly and religious life and in the service of the Church, to mark the 175th anniversary of the Archdiocese of Freiburg (1827-2002).

Grateful thanks also to the authors for permission to use the following prayers:
Page 42: *I am nothing without you,* Alfons Höfer, S.J.
Page 115: *On the road of life,* Klaus Nagorni.

For some of the prayers used in this book it was not possible, despite careful research, to identify the author.

## A word of thanks...

...to all the young people who helped by praying and reading through the above texts with us and giving us their critical advice and opinion.

**Photo Credits**
Cecilia Engels, 116; Congregation of Franciscan Srs. in Sießen, 95; Alexander Lengerke, 6, 10–11, 45, 61, 84, 146, 163; Felix Löwenstein, 127; Fr. Leo Maasburg, 144; Antoinette Mirbach-Harff, 25; Ricardo Perna, 36, 82, 114, 141; Luc Serafin, 16, 19, 28, 49, 53, 57, 80, 86, 92, 100–101, 122, 128, 136, 142, 151, 160
Inside covers: Michaela Heereman, Christoph Hurnaus (www.papstfoto.com), YOUCAT-Institut (www.youcat.org)

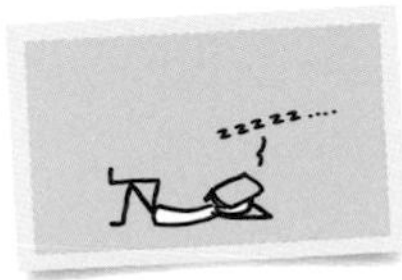